RAILWAYS ROUND THE CHILTERNS

Dr Rudi Newman

PiXZ

Dr Rudi Newman has a long-standing passion for all things historical, particularly in his specialist field of transportation. Having previously researched various maritime themes, his PhD centred on Victorian railways and their early impacts. A collector of transportation ephemera supporting his historical research, he has assisted with museums and exhibitions on a range of related subject matters and has presented numerous lectures and articles on transportation themes. He has also acted as a media advisor and been featured in numerous documentaries and interviews in Britain and across Europe.

To the countless men and women who built and ran the railways,
their actions helping forge the world of today.

Images marked * are included under
Creative Commons Attribution Share-alike licenses 2.0-4.0.

The Author wishes to thank in particular the generosity of
David Begley, Pam Borthwick, Owen Chapman, Peter Hodge,
Mike Izzard, Trevor Monk, Simon Mulligan, Rebecca Press, Jane Reilly
and Ashley Richards in sharing their photographs and expertise.

First published in Great Britain in 2022

British Library Cataloguing-in-Publication Data.
A CIP record for this title is available from the British Library.

ISBN 978 0 85710 131 0

PiXZ Books
Halsgrove House, Ryelands Business Park, Bagley Road, Wellington,
Somerset TA21 9PZ Tel: 01823 653777
Fax: 01823 216796
email: sales@halsgrove.com

An imprint of Halstar Ltd, part of the Halsgrove group of companies.
Information on all Halsgrove titles is available at: www.halsgrove.com.

Printed and bound in India by Parksons Graphics Pvt Ltd

Contents

GWR railmotor No. 93; many branches used similar units to economise with quicker turnaround times improving efficiency – Author, with permission from Didcot Railway Centre.

The Railways of the Chilterns

Hertfordshire, Bedfordshire & Buckinghamshire

Abbreviations Used

BoT	Board of Trade
BTC	British Transport Commission
DMU	Diesel Multiple Unit
EMU	Electric Multiple Unit
EWJR	East & West Junction Railway
GJR	Grand Junction Railway
LMR	Liverpool & Manchester Railway
MoD	Ministry of Defence

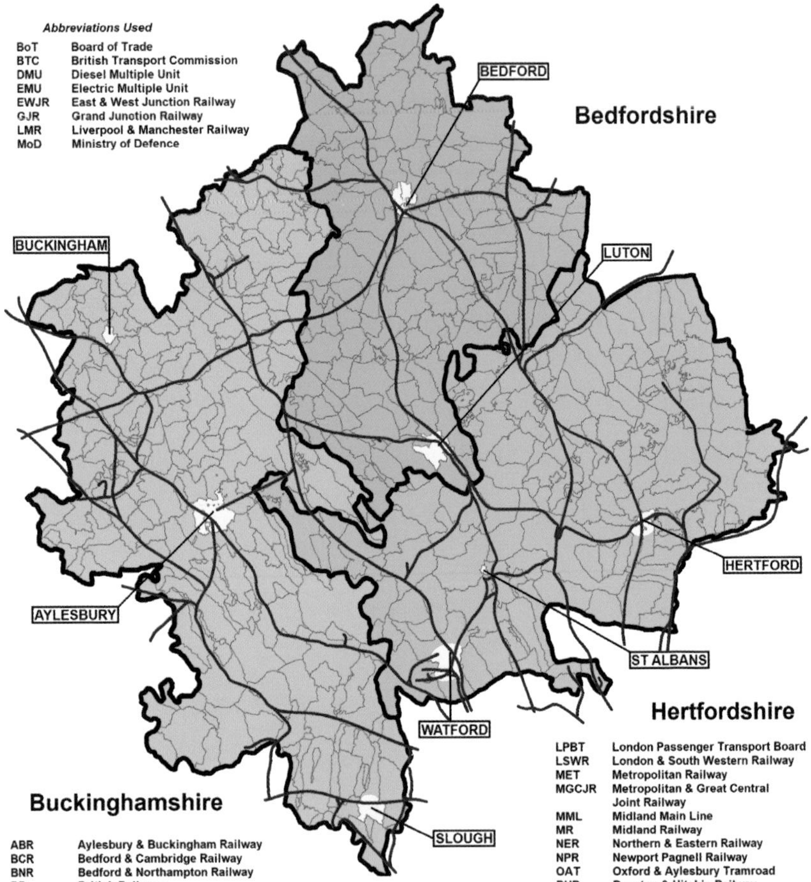

ABR	Aylesbury & Buckingham Railway
BCR	Bedford & Cambridge Railway
BNR	Bedford & Northampton Railway
BR	British Railways
BuckR	Buckinghamshire Railway
ECML	East Coast Main Line
ECR	Eastern Counties Railway
GCR	Great Central Railway
GER	Great Eastern Railway
GNR	Great Northern Railway
GWGCJR	Great Western & Great Central Joint Railway
GWR	Great Western Railway
HStAR	Hatfield & St Albans Railway
LBR	London & Birmingham Railway
LDWJR	Luton, Dunstable & Welwyn Junction Railway
LNER	London & North Eastern Railway
LMS	London Midland & Scottish Railway
LNWR	London & North Western Railway
LPBT	London Passenger Transport Board
LSWR	London & South Western Railway
MET	Metropolitan Railway
MGCJR	Metropolitan & Great Central Joint Railway
MML	Midland Main Line
MR	Midland Railway
NER	Northern & Eastern Railway
NPR	Newport Pagnell Railway
OAT	Oxford & Aylesbury Tramroad
RHR	Royston & Hitchin Railway
SMJR	Stratford-upon-Avon & Midland Junction Railway
SPR	Sandy & Potton Railway
SR	Southern Railway
TFL	Transport for London
WCML	West Coast Main Line
WHBR	Ware, Hadham & Buntingford Railway
WR	Wycombe Railway

A Chiltern Overview

The counties of Hertfordshire, Bedfordshire and Buckinghamshire, encircling the Chiltern Hills, have long played a major part in national history. A key element has been transportation, both through traversing these hills and their position around north London – a gateway to the Capital. Featuring roads, waterways and even aircraft companies, it was another form that particularly stood out: the railways.

From 1838 to 1925 some 45 networked lines were built across this region by 35 individual companies. Each has its own history reflecting elements of rail development. The first were in days when railways were still a new technology, something to be feared. As their success and profitability became clear this turned to enthusiasm – exemplified by the three great 'Railway Manias'. Some lines built were indeed necessary, but others stemmed from rampant competition or civic pride with settlements clamouring for a station. Remarkably, only one third of all proposals were actually built – potentially worsening what was already a convoluted tangle of lines.

While the earliest railways focused on destinations over intermediate regions, as company rivalries and increasing track mileage led to improved services so these counties saw mounting impacts. Passenger traffic ranged from daily commuting (ever-increasing with growing rail access) to more permanent rural-urban migration. Agriculture provided much goods traffic, and while industry was initially limited it prospered with railway provision. Their impacts on local settlements could vary substantially, not only in population, occupation and urbanisation but equally in extent. Wolverton Works was the epicenter of the town, initially utterly dependent on the whims of the railway. Quainton, only a few miles away, was a notable junction but conversely remained a sleepy village. The railways were a factor in creating these effects, but these in turn affected the railways, so continually fuelling change over the years. Then there were those settlements that never gained a connection or that were later to lose them. The result is a patchwork of different interactions, developments and consequences that show the true value behind the railways.

The Chilterns has a lengthy history, its railways playing an important role in that local chronology. This introduction presents every railway in the area that was part of the national network – some large and nationally important, others small and scarcely remembered. Whether running to this day or just a distant memory, they helped make the Chilterns what it is today, and tell of the railways' role in the transformation of Britain.

Footplate of MET No. 1 – Author, with permission from the Buckinghamshire Railway Centre.

1: Main lines

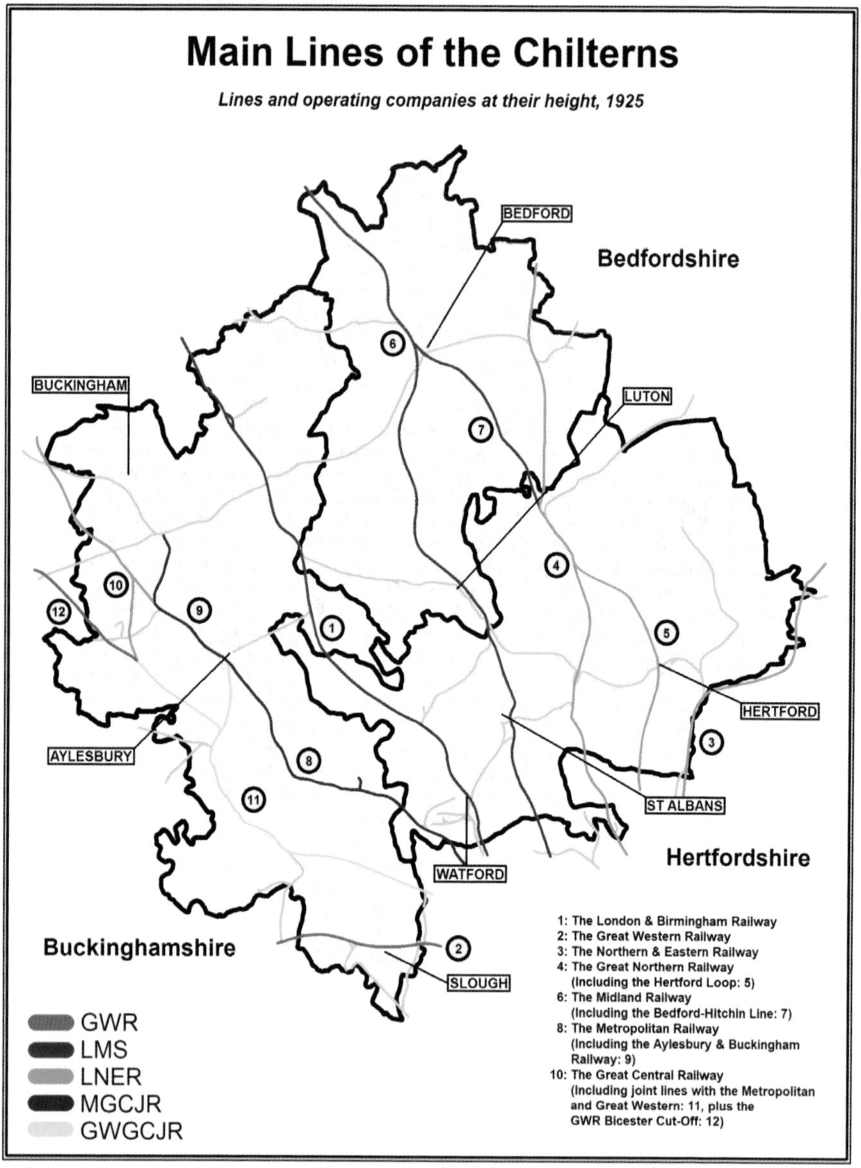

Main Lines of the Chilterns
Lines and operating companies at their height, 1925
BEDFORD
Bedfordshire
LUTON
BUCKINGHAM
HERTFORD
AYLESBURY
ST ALBANS
WATFORD
Hertfordshire
Buckinghamshire
SLOUGH
1: The London & Birmingham Railway
2: The Great Western Railway
3: The Northern & Eastern Railway
4: The Great Northern Railway
(Including the Hertford Loop: 5)
6: The Midland Railway
(Including the Bedford-Hitchin Line: 7)
8: The Metropolitan Railway
(Including the Aylesbury & Buckingham Railway: 9)
10: The Great Central Railway
(Including joint lines with the Metropolitan and Great Western: 11, plus the GWR Bicester Cut-Off: 12)
GWR
LMS
LNER
MGCJR
GWGCJR

Britain's railways fall into three primary categories, the most significant being national main lines of which the Chilterns were but a small part. Incorporating the pivotal lines of three of the 'Big Four' railway companies, there was also one of the few to have succumbed to 1960s closures and its one-time partner – unique to the Chilterns and itself a London icon. With a combined distance of over 300 miles, remaining some of the most significant transport routes in Britain, their histories introduce the key companies pivotal to every other Chiltern railway.

The London & Birmingham Railway

The success of the 1830 'Liverpool & Manchester Railway' (LMR) demonstrated the feasibility of rail travel, interest turning to new routes. Foremost was a main 'trunk' line to London – a world first – which in turn sparked ever-faster railway expansion. Becoming part of a vital national artery, its later history reflects broader changes in rail practices.

♦ *Dogged Determination*

Rather than a single pre-planned network the earliest lines only intended to join specific locations, and a connection between London and industrial Birmingham was an obvious choice. In 1823 engineer John Rennie proposed a line via Oxford and Banbury, shortly followed by Francis Giles with a rival plan through Coventry. Neither had great support, so they united to form a stronger proposition: the 'London & Birmingham Railway' (LBR). Several routes were considered, famed engineers George and Robert Stephenson appointed to survey plans, with Robert becoming its chief engineer. Unfortunately opposition was marked, from landowners to canal and turnpike road companies, and its first Bill was rejected by Parliament. Undaunted, an Act was successfully passed in 1833 with a Hertfordshire route terminating at Camden, extended to Euston (as originally intended) in 1835.

Construction began on 1 June 1834 in an unparalleled project. However, further deviations were forced on the LBR through landowner campaigning, this included meetings at Berkhampstead and Watford. Of particular impact were the Cassiobury and Grove estates at Watford, seats of the Earls of Essex and Clarendon. Blocking railway access the line had to dog-leg to the east, forcing construction of several viaducts, embankments and the Watford Tunnel – all previously unnecessary. Hostility was not limited to the aristocracy; farmers were also aggrieved as recorded by F.R. Condor of the LBR's Watford survey:

> *'The Farmers, naturally indignant, ordered these intruders from their fields. The engineers, for such they were, took but little notice. The farmers proceeded to threats. The ringleader of the invaders produced a red book, folded in an oblong form, from the voluminous pocket of his velveteen jacket, and offered it to the irate farmer as a sedative, informing him that it was the Act of Parliament by authority of which he was acting...One thing alone remained for them* [the farmers] *to do...they would shoot the intruders. But the latter calmly replied that that was no business of theirs, and the farmers did not draw trigger...'*

Rails finally crossed Cassiobury with the 1959 Watford Miniature Railway – S. Mulligan.

Opening in sections, the first train left Euston to Boxmoor (Hemel Hempstead) on 20 July 1837. Running three trains daily, the first 28 days saw 38,855 passengers – many travelling simply for curiosity. Previously on 13 July a Directors special was run, ingloriously crashing into the Euston 'receiving house' injuring 12 as the guard had turned the brake wheel the wrong way... Extended to Tring by 16 October, from 9 April 1838 services ran to a temporary terminus at Denbigh Hall near Bletchley. Birmingham to Rugby also opened that day, but their connection was delayed by the Kilsby Tunnel (Northamptonshire). The full line finally opened on 17 September 1838, reducing London-Birmingham journey times from c.2.5 days by stagecoach to under six hours.

Further developments began almost immediately. Not anticipating intermediate traffic (initially focussing on terminus-terminus trade), demand led to additional stations and local services particularly with growing populations between Euston and Watford. Broadening its reach, agreements were formed with other companies including the Manchester-Birmingham 'Grand Junction Railway' (GJR), and in 1842 it helped found the 'Railway Clearing House': an organisation distributing revenue from cross-company tickets. Competition remained a serious issue, however, the GJR taking advantage by supporting a rival Oxford-Birmingham proposal directly competing with the LBR (p.37). Such was its risk (alongside other competing plans) that the LBR had to capitulate to a GJR-desired amalgamation, they and the 'Manchester & Birmingham Railway' forming the 'London & North Western Railway' (LNWR) on 16 July 1846.

LMS Pride: Stanier No. 6201 Princess Elizabeth *crossing the 'Five Arches' at Watford – O. Chapman.*

The LNWR grew into a formidable company stretching as far as Carlisle and Holyhead. The ex-LBR was at its core, particularly after agreement with the 1848 'Caledonian Railway' enabled London-Edinburgh services. Nicknamed the 'Premier Line', this would form today's *West Coast Main Line* (WCML). An early Chairman (1853-61) was the Marquess of Chandos, later Third Duke of Buckingham. Famously scruffy, the day he was elected a clerk unknowingly declared him not fit to be a porter...!

The Chilterns section, part of the LNWR's 'Southern Division' until 1862, witnessed marked changes to cope with increasing London-bound traffic. An additional 'goods relief' line was built from Primrose Hill to Watford in 1858, extended to Bletchley in 1859. Intended to free the main line from slow London-bound goods trains it was briefly used for passengers in 1886 until an accident at the Watford Tunnel. This expanded further, an 1872 Act authorising quadrupling of the line. Watford-Bletchley was completed in 1874, to Leighton by 1876 and the entire Euston-Rugby portion finished by 1882.

♦ *The Route*

The LBR was 112 miles from Euston to Birmingham, c.39 miles weaving northwest through Hertfordshire and northern Buckinghamshire. Wanting the flattest route Stephenson largely followed the 'Grand Junction Canal' (GJC) to maintain low gradients, one of the steeper being a mere 1 in 335 around Berkhamsted, but consequently required heavy civil engineering such as the Wolverton Viaduct. Heading north stations included Bushey & Oxhey (1841; renamed Bushey 1974 but strangely also known as 'Ampersand' during WWII owing to a bureaucratic error in redacting all bar the '&' from signage), Watford ('Watford Junction' from

1858), Kings Langley (1839; named 'Kings Langley & Abbots Langley'1909-74), Apsley (1938), Boxmoor (renamed 'Boxmoor & Hemel Hempstead' 1912, 'Hemel Hempstead & Boxmoor' 1930 and 'Hemel Hempstead' 1963), Berkhamsted, Tring, Cheddington ('Aylesbury Junction' 1838 and 'Cheddington Junction' c.1850-70), Leighton (renamed 'Leighton Buzzard' 1911), Bletchley ('Bletchley & Fenny Stratford' 1841-6 and 'Bletchley Junction' 1851-70), Milton Keynes Central (1982), Wolverton (originally 'New Wolverton') and Castlethorpe (1882, closed 1964).

Still used for access, the original LBR track through Wolverton Works (bypassed in 1883) – Author.

♦ *Wolverton*

The first LBR engines were Edward Bury designs only able to carry coke and water for half the line's length. The main Works was therefore located centrally – Wolverton (Buckinghamshire). Built from scratch as the world's first planned 'railway town', everything depended on the company from employment and housing to shops, pubs and even Britain's first railway-funded church. Locomotive manufacture commenced in 1845, peaking under James McConnell with his 'Bloomer' express engines, but this moved to Crewe in 1864 with Wolverton becoming the centre for carriage manufacture. Famously the home of the Royal Train, Queen Victoria was personally involved with its design. Wolverton set a benchmark of excellence, even purportedly inventing the gas pilot light, and such was its importance to the railway that Chairman George Glynn was made the first modern 'Baronet of Wolverton'.

The town grew in relation to the ever-expanding Works, landowner difficulties ver new housing triggering satellite settlements connected by a branch (p.113) nd tramway. The original main line ran through the Works, creating a bottleneck uring track quadrupling, so Chairman Richard Moon proposed the 'Wolverton oop': an eastern bypass. Nicknamed 'Moon's Folly', it was completed with the own's third station site in 1882. Expanding further, during WWI 'ambulance rains' were built for continental use, in WWII producing wooden RAF components notably 'Horsa' gliders for D-Day. 1950s cutbacks culminated with carriage nanufacture ceasing in 1962, becoming repair-only. Passing through firms post-rivatisation, still housing the Royal Train and becoming the world's oldest ontinually-used railway works, in 2016 the reduced site was threatened with losure. While still at risk, workshop expansion plans in the early 2020s, however, uggest that hopefully a rail-based future remains for this historic location.

Castles, Crashes and Crime

Vhile landowner difficulties hindered construction, one instance would have najor future repercussions. Site of the surrender of England to William the Conqueror, Berkhamsted Castle lay guarding a narrow valley. The only flat oute, already accommodating the GJC and road, the LBR intended to build traight through the site destroying its ruins. While the Duke of Bridgewater vanted to protect his scenery, there was also growing concern over the lack f protection for historic monuments. The LBR's 1833 Act therefore expressly rotected the castle, forcing a change in route. Although the line moved only a ew yards away, still destroying the Castle's gatehouse, it was a key precedent: the rst British building to have legal protection for its historic merits. Opposition imilarly led to the farcical 'Battle of Wolverton'. Requiring a temporary bridge ver the GJC, the canal contested their rights. Rather than delay, Stephenson ad the bridge erected by torchlight on 23 December 1834, completed on Christmas Day. Canal workers retaliated, demolishing the entire structure on 0 December. The matter was only finally resolved by an injunction from the Court of Chancery...

McConnell's Wolverton engines were highly successful, but his first was more mbarrassing. Built in 1848 No. 227 had outside frames and outside cylinders, naking it particularly wide. Locomotive and Permanent Way departments did ot interact at this time, and the passing engine promptly destroyed platform dges. Forced to modify each platform, the engine was nicknamed 'Mac's Mangle'!

The WCML has seen accidents, Watford in particular suffering several. mongst others, on 23 January 1975 a passenger service struck stillages fallen rom a previous goods train. Derailed, another train struck it and fell down ne embankment with one fatality and 11 injured. Then on 8 August 1996 a rain overshot a danger signal, being struck by another oncoming passenger ervice that had been authorised to cross tracks, with one killed and 69 injured. here was a close shave, conversely, on 3 February 1954 when a broken rail t the Watford Tunnel derailed an express, part-mounting the platform. While

16 were injured, there were no fatalities. Similarly, a landslide at the Tunnel or 16 September 2016 caused a derailment and collision with an oncoming trair but amazingly with no injuries.

Sometimes railways endure criminal actions; the 1963 Great Train Robber near Leighton Buzzard being an infamous example. Lesser-known is a plo occurring at Bushey on 13 September 1880. A platelayer inspecting the trac found two fishplates removed and a parcel with rubber tubing. Inside, he thought was red lead pigment The Bushey Stationmaste called for Euston detectives later joined by local anc Metropolitan Police plu the railway's regiona head. Instead of pigment the contents were fou pounds of dynamite – th tubing gunpower-fillec with a percussion cap t be detonated by a passin train. Fortunately vibratior had caused it to fall clea but the incident becam international news. Motives were suggested, most probably Irish radical targeting the London-Holyhead Irish Mail, but despite a £100 reward nobod was ever caught...

Bushey water troughs, publicised in an LNWR postcard – Author's Collection.

♦ *The 'Big Four' and Beyond*

During WWI Britain's railways were temporarily government-run, and permanent post-war reorganisation of the c.120 British railway companie became necessary to limit competition and financial losses. Rather than ful nationalisation they were grouped into four companies by the Railways Act 1921 Coming into effect on 1 January 1923, the LNWR became part of the 'Londo Midland & Scottish Railway' (LMS) – the world's largest single transport compan with over 7,100 miles by 1938. Becoming important not just as a commercia route but for LMS self-promotion, competition continued particularly agains the *East Coast Main Line* (ECML) culminating in the 1937 *Coronation Scot* service

WWII overstretched Britain's railways and, unable to realistically rais sufficient funding privately, the Government sought nationalisation throug the Transport Act 1947. On 1 January 1948 this created the 'British Transpor Commission' (BTC), under which fell 'British Railways' (BR). Part of wide post-war nationalisation but doomed to financial failure, the BTC was in tur replaced with the 'British Railways Board' from 1963. The LMS, however, onl ceased to exist on 23 December 1949 (as with the other 'Big Four' companies when its tracks officially became the 'London Midland' Region. WCML operatio continued, only significantly changing with the 1955 BR 'Modernisation Plan

Ieralding the end of steam, electrification was undertaken in stages towards .ondon, trains running hourly from 18 April 1966. With improved speed and requency passenger numbers doubled c.1962-75.

Known as 'British Rail' from 1965, sectorisation in 1982 ended the former Regions, instead using 'InterCity' for expresses and from 1986 'Network .outhEast' for London commuter services. In 1994 Privatisation commenced, operation transferring to individual franchises from 1996. WCML improvements continued, notably infrastructure for high-speed tilting trains completed in 2008. With expresses under 'Avanti West Coast' from 2019, in 2017 London suburban ervices came under 'London Northwestern Railway', named for its illustrious predecessor. Having operated for over 180 years, with relics of its origins still in daily use, today the WCML remains of great significance to Britain's network.

The Great Western Railway

The LBR was swiftly joined by other cross-country lines. Just within Buckinghamshire, this route remains one of Britain's most iconic railways; the sole pre-Grouping company to retain its identity. Cementing the reputation of its designer, his decisions, however, created major challenges.

A New Type of Railway

By the 1830s trade with America was booming. As Liverpool Port rose, particularly with rail connections, its rival Bristol sought its own London link. Initial plans failed, but a public meeting on 21 January 1833 founded the 'Bristol and London Railroad', in August renamed the 'Great Western Railway' (GWR). Hiring the little-known engineer Isambard Kingdom Brunel, landowner opposition forced modifications, particularly around Oxford University, Eton College and Windsor Castle. Limited funds meant their 1834 Bill was not even for the complete railway, and it was rejected by Parliament. An Act was successfully passed in 1835, but Brunel took advantage of the reapplication by removing a vital clause – track gauge. Highly critical of the traditional 4-foot 8.5-inch width (later 'standard gauge'), he calculated a 7-foot 0.25-inch optimum ('broad gauge', although the GWR insisted on calling it 'standard'!) enabling greater stability at higher speeds with additional space for larger boilers and more carrying capacity. The two gauges were, however, completely incompatible – a troubling portent.

Replica broad-gauge locomotive Fire Fly – *Author, with permission from Didcot Railway Centre.*

Built in sections, following a Directors special the first train ran from

Paddington to Taplow (Buckinghamshire) on 4 June 1838. It was extended t Twyford (Berkshire) on 1 July 1839 and Reading on 30 March 1840, finall completed with the Box Tunnel (Wiltshire) on 30 June 1841. An 1836 Ac permitted a terminus at Paddington (previously considering Euston – blocke by the LBR – or Vauxhall Bridge), the completed station opening in 1854. Ther were initial problems with underpowered locomotives and settling track, plu ballooning costs, but the line made Brunel a household name. Expansion bega almost immediately, at its height the GWR covering most of Wales and southwes England. The first line with regular 50mph running, passenger revenue wa great – particularly with improved provisions in the wake of the 1844 Railwa Regulation Act 'parliamentary trains'. Goods were initially limited but as Wels and Midland mines became more accessible it rose to be a major revenue source.

The Plymouth-Paddington 100mph record-breaker City of Truro – *Author, with permission from Didcot Railway Centre.*

But success was to be tempered. The different gauges made inconvenient transhipment necessary where meeting, growing competition for 'territory' forcing new railways to adopt one gauge or the other – polarising company loyalties and fuelling arguments over which should become the standard. Known as the 'Battle of the Gauges', a Royal Commission was established in 1845 to decide the issue. Engine tests showed broad gauge superiority, but a visit to Glouceste famously revealed the mayhem of transhipment (actually falsely contrived b the anti-GWR goods manager). With less broad gauge mileage nationally, th Commission was obliged to support the narrower as 'standard', banning norther broad gauge construction. Isolated, piecemeal adoption of a third rail for dua gauge operation proved necessary. Agreement with the 'West Midland Railwa (p.64) resulted in such conversion of the London-Reading section in 1861 an by 1875 most trains were standard gauge. Cornwall remained the exceptio its London services still including broad gauge trains. After his death Brunel system finally succumbed, the last broad gauge train departing Paddington o 20 May 1892.

♦ *The Route*

118 miles long from Paddington to Bristol, c.10 miles crossing west-east throug southernmost Buckinghamshire, Brunel insisted on the flattest route possibl Gradients here were a miniscule 1 in 1320 – but the indirect snaking route led t nicknames of the 'Great Way Round' or 'Brunel's billiard table'. Stations headin west were at Iver (1924), Langley (1845), Slough (unofficially 1838, officiall

1840 after Eton limitations were repealed), Burnham (1899 as 'Burnham Beeches', temporarily closed 1917-19, renamed 'Burnham (Bucks)' 1930-75), Taplow (originally 'Maidenhead', then 'Maidenhead & Taplow' 1854-71) and Maidenhead (1871).

♦ *Monuments and Murder*

Formerly within Buckinghamshire (now Berkshire), the Maidenhead Bridge is an engineering triumph. Constrained by river clearance and his desire for a flat route, Brunel created the flattest arches ever built but encountered critical responses. Claims of instability appeared true when the arches began to settle – actually the fault of un-set mortar – and when completed in 1838 the supporting timber framework was kept in place. Brunel, however, knew this was unnecessary so had these supports minutely lowered, removing any supportive function. Washed away in bad weather, the bridge stood unaided and Brunel was vindicated, trains running over it from 1 July 1839.

Also formerly Buckinghamshire, Slough Station has witnessed notable criminal events. The largest drug seizure by British Transport Police occurred there in 2009, but more significant was the case of John Tawell. Married, Tawell was having an affair with nurse Sarah Hart but struggled to finance the illicit relationship. On 1 January 1845 he poisoned her beer with Prussic Acid, fleeing the scene when her screams were overheard. At Slough Station Tawell caught a train, supposedly escaping. However, the new electric telegraph apparatus was used to send a message to Paddington, informing the police who tailed and subsequently arrested him. Tried and executed, this was the first time a murderer had been caught using the electric telegraph – a message could now outpace a train. Proving the value of the technology, the basis of today's wireless communication, for years after the system was known as 'the cords that hanged John Tawell'...

Maidenhead Bridge, c.1880 – Author's Collection.

No. 4087 Cardigan Castle *passes through Slough, 1959 – B. Brooksbank*.*

♦ *Consolidation and Continuation*

Broad gauge had fallen but the GWR prospered. Excursions grew in popularity from the 1850s, Cornish tourism leading to the 1908 moniker of the 'Holiday Line'. Aided by introduction of 'Automatic Train Control' after an accident at Slough in 1900, speeds increased alongside a glowing safety record – the 1930s' *Cheltenham Flyer* the world's fastest commercial service. Further improvements included quadrupling the main line, completed to Slough in June 1879, Maidenhead Bridge in May 1884 and Reading by June 1893. 1883-5 even briefly saw 'District Railway' underground trains serve main line stations towards Windsor.

Under the Grouping the GWR expanded in scale and public image, surviving the 1926 General Strike and the Depression. WWII saw particular use of the Chiltern stretch, Taplow Station aiding in transporting tanks, but the War severely weakened the company. Nationalisation was strongly resisted, but nonetheless it became the core of BR's Western Region. Rivalries continued against the ex-LMS and the Region retained some operational independence, in 1966 becoming the first to completely end steam traction. By the 1970s upgrades were made for greater speeds, while operations transferred to 'Great Western Trains' under Privatisation. From 2015 this returned to the traditional name 'Great Western Railway'. Excepting a short London section in 1998 electrification only commenced in 2011, completed across Buckinghamshire c.2017 and to Bristol by December 2018. Brunel's legacy remains, and with plans for Crossrail connections through to Reading its national value will only grow.

The Northern & Eastern Railway

Success for fledgling railways was not guaranteed, financial backing proving a key hurdle. Today's *West Anglia Main Line* reflects the resultant challenges, nearly destroying its operators and curtailing grander plans. Undergoing significant changes, its route nonetheless formed the spine of a substantial rural network.

Sawbridgeworth Station, 2010 – G. Canny.*

♦ *Fraught Origins*

As railways developed Cambridge, a notable agricultural and rising industrial location, became a coveted target, but early attempts came to naught. Then on 23 January 1836 a public meeting in Cambridge formed the 'Northern & Eastern Railway' (NER), proposing a London-Cambridge line plus extensions to Lincoln and Yarmouth via Norwich. By its assent in July 1836, however, this had shrunk to just Cambridge – the first of many reductions. Unlike Birmingham or Bristol the rural area meant funding was limited, causing ongoing problems. The intended Islington terminus required an expensive tunnel, so discussions led to use of the 1840 London-Ipswich 'Eastern Counties Railway' (ECR) Shoreditch terminus (renamed Bishopsgate in 1846), the two lines meeting at Stratford. Following the GWR, the ECR rejected standard gauge, instead adopting 5-foot gauge (cheaper than broad gauge), and as such the NER had to use the same. Construction commenced in 1837 under engineer Michael Borthwick, but finances were a continual hindrance. Contractor difficulties led to Robert Stephenson being brought in as consulting 'Engineer in Chief', while noted contractors Grissell & Peto took over work in stages from 1840. That year another Act abandoned the intended line from Bishop's Stortford (Hertfordshire) to Cambridge. Worsened by an annual £7,000 terminus rent (plus tolls per passenger), finances had crippled the NER's original intentions.

Operated by the ECR, a Directors special to Broxbourne (as temporary terminus) ran on 12 September 1840, opening to the public with decorations on 15 September. This first portion was single track, doubled in 1841, with services running through to Shoreditch as the London stations remained exclusive to the ECR. Following sections opened to Harlow and Spellbrook in 1841 and finally Bishop's Stortford on 16 May 1842. Initial operations were promising, so under an 1843 Act the NER looked to extend to Newport (Essex) heading towards Cambridge. Financially overstretched as a result, in 1844 an Act leased the railway to the ECR, the NER henceforth becoming but a shell. Recognising the growing importance of through traffic conversion immediately began to standard gauge, from 5 September to 7 October 1844 without any late trains. The ECR continued building northwards, expanding to Newport, Cambridge and Ely, then on 30 July 1845 to Brandon (Norfolk) meeting another line to Norwich and Yarmouth. Now completed, further connections developed, notably to Kings Lynn and Ipswich. Constructing and acquiring other lines, despite its own initial plan being truncated the ECR ultimately developed a network spanning most of East Anglia.

Holden's Claud Hamilton *express locomotive – Author's Collection.*

Unfortunately this all placed additional burden on the ECR, which was itself financially unsound. With revenue failing to reach expectations the company turned to railway financier George Hudson, the so-dubbed 'Railway King', who became Chairman in October 1845. Finances appeared to recover, extensions were proposed and dividends increased, but this was short-lived. A low dividend in 1849 led to increasingly-wary shareholders initiating an investigation, discovering that traffic accounts had been falsified to reflect Hudson's inflated dividends. Resigning, by 1853 Hudson was disgraced and many railways nation-wide damaged by association. The ECR suffered further with Chairman David Waddington (formerly Hudson's vice-chairman) being dismissed in 1856 for fraud.

♦ *Amalgamation*

Damaged by these misadventures, financial economies further hampered operation. Conflict with other companies, distrust within joint committees and ever-weak finances placed it in a critical position, many looking to amalgamation as a solution. This had been a long-term government condition of permitting the ECR to lease most Anglian lines, but Parliament conversely preferred to encourage competition over potential monopoly. An amalgamation bill was only therefore presented in 1861, authorised after lengthy debate in 1862. Six companies merged forming the 'Great Eastern Railway' (GER), although the NER tracks technically remained independently-owned until acquired in 1902.

Improved services and greater efficiency raised revenue, finances beginning to stabilise by 1863-4. Expansion was again considered, but an 1865 article in *The Times* wrecked this advancement. Citing director disagreements, management problems surfaced resulting in an investigation finding unauthorised loans and detrimental leases. Recovery under a new board struggled, worsened by the 1866 post-'Mania' depression, and after attempting to gain further loans on 2 July 1867 the GER was put into receivership. Fortunately this was brief, the company recovering by August 1869 thanks to Sir Edward Watkin and Viscount Cranborne (of Hatfield House, Hertfordshire; later the Third Marquis of Salisbury and Prime Minister). Finally stable, improvements restarted with a shortened inner-London route in 1872 (p.137) and a new terminus at Liverpool Street in 1874-5. 1880s access to Yorkshire via the 'Great Northern Railway' (GNR) boosted coal traffic in particular, while an agreement with the 'Midland Railway' (MR) saw GER passenger trains using St Pancras c.1870-1917. Track quadrupling was considered c.1900 but later cancelled, although further upgrades were made to meet WWI traffic demands (moving some 10.5 million servicemen).

♦ *The Route*

Totalling 55 miles from Liverpool Street to Cambridge, c.32 miles of double track skirted the eastern Hertfordshire border zig-zagging northwest along the Lea Valley. Using a twisting route rather than civil engineering to keep gradients low through the Chiltern Hills, the line consequently entered Essex in places. Hertfordshire stations heading north served Waltham Cross ('Waltham' 1840-82 and 'Waltham Cross & Abbey' 1894-1969), Cheshunt (closed 1842-6), Broxbourne ('Broxbourne Junction' from 1843), Sawbridgeworth (1841) and Bishop's Stortford ('Stortford' 1842-5). A temporary excursion station at Hockerill was also used in 1843-4.

♦ *Debts and Danger*

The ECR increasingly faltered as a company, its association with the disgraced Hudson one of many factors. By the 1850s its financial position led to corner-cutting, gaining a reputation for being slow, dirty and dangerous. Just as bad, fares grew 20-25% higher than competitors, these short-term actions hampering long-term traffic. *Punch* magazine often mocked the company, once jesting that a sixteen-year-old with a child's ticket defended themselves saying they were twelve when the journey started! Finances failed to improve under the GER, falling under the Court of Chancery by 1867. Lenders even began reclaiming assets – some locomotives carrying plates declaring their new creditor owners! Keen to turn things around, Watkin became a director and recommended a new Board and Chairman: fellow MP Viscount Cranborne. Cranborne had been reticent to accept, being somewhat cajoled into it, but from his start in 1868 he proved highly skilled. Unfamiliar with railway operation, he quickly learnt and

Broxbourne Station, 1960 – B. Brooksbank.*

was actively involved in all aspects of the business. Unusually he was strongly anti-competition, considering it potentially damaging and against the public interest. His impact was marked: GER finances were turned around, leaving Chancery and even paying a small dividend. This was despite his predecessor Charles Turner (acting as Vice-Chair) defrauding the GER of £38,000! His work complete, Cranborne (now Lord Salisbury) was happy to leave and pass the Chair to Watkin. The shareholders, however, disagreed and it was only in 1871 on his third attempt that Salisbury stepped down. Watkin left in August 1872, having been offered chairmanship of the 'Metropolitan Railway' (MET).

The General Strike caused massive national upheaval, volunteers maintaining essential services. Railway complexities were a challenge though, leading to disaster. On 10 May 1926, just before the strike ceased, a goods train passed a red signal and struck the rear of a Cambridge-London stopping train stationary at Bishop Stortford Station. Carriages telescoped and 170 feet of the platform canopy collapsed, killing one and injuring three. The volunteer goods driver had assumed the line was clear and misjudged his speed, so undoing the 'time interval' system in operation. Dangerous in itself, its temporary use over 'block signalling' was due to the lack of signalmen during the Strike. Ironically volunteers began using the safer 'block' system the very next day.

♦ *The LNER to Today*

Becoming part of the 'London & North Eastern Railway' (LNER) under the Grouping, the Broxbourne line was eclipsed by the ex-GNR Royston-Cambridge route (p.93), but suburban traffic remained strong. Goods was similarly major until the 1950s. Transferring to BR's Eastern Region, this was in turn subdivided in 1957 with partial ex-GER autonomy, dieselisation beginning shortly thereafter. However, in March 1963 Dr Richard Beeching published his infamous report *The Reshaping of British Railways*. Best known for closing branch lines it also

A4 No. 4464 Bittern, *dwarfed by the Digswell Viaduct – O. Chapman.*

featured passenger service 'modifications'. Bishops Stortford-Cambridge was included, although London-Cambridge train frequency actually increased from 1960. Piecemeal electrification occurred with Broxbourne reached that year, extended to Bishops Stortford on 9 March 1969, and under 'Network SouthEast' to Cambridge on 19 January 1987. Following Privatisation it was operated by 'Anglia Railways', merging into the 'Greater Anglia' franchise in 2004. Plans for track quadrupling up to Broxbourne as part of the proposed 'Crossrail 2' project were shelved due to the 2020 COVID-19 pandemic, so despite survival and stabilisation its history of curtailed aspirations may yet threaten to repeat itself…

The Great Northern Railway

As the 'Manias' triggered expansion, the West Coast Main Line soon faced competition. One of the most serious was from today's East Coast Main Line, essentially a rail equivalent of the Great North Road offering an alternate Scottish route. Facing substantial challenges and sparking decades of rivalry it nonetheless prospered and remains a major national artery.

♦ *A New Route North*

The first plan for a London-York railway began c.1836 but, overambitious, swiftly failed. The notion reappeared in 1845 with several proposals competing with each other as well as encountering external opponents. So many railways were proposed during this second 'Mania' that a Board of Trade (BoT) committee dubbed the 'Five Kings' was formed to advise, while ongoing opposition from George Hudson (defending his control of railways around York) deliberately stretched proceedings until the Parliamentary session ran out. As other proposals collapsed so supporters joined forces under the 'London & York Railway', overcoming BoT criticism (being already on its second reading before Parliament) and rejecting an offer from Hudson of ECR shares if the Bill was dropped. Such were the numbers at the hearings that one clerk particularly noted the attending supporters' smell! Reflecting the merged groups the proposal was renamed the 'Great Northern Railway' (GNR), gaining assent in 1846.

These delays were not without damage. Parliamentary expenses forced cost-cutting: rather than build its own line to York it instead met the 1841 'Great North of England Railway' (from 1854 part of the 'North Eastern Railway') at

Askern near Doncaster, sharing their line north. Significantly delays meant work only began after the 'Mania's collapse, investment thus decreasing. Forced to prioritise finances, focus turned to a Lincolnshire loop line rather than the direct Doncaster-Peterborough 'Towns Line', the first GNR train (on a leased line) running on 1 March 1848. Extending southwards in stages, the Peterborough-London stretch built by engineer Joseph Cubitt (under father William) and well-known contractor Thomas Brassey opened with a demonstration train on 5 August 1850. Public services commenced two day later and goods from 12 December. Using a temporary terminus at Maiden Lane, the direct 'Towns Line' and Kings Cross were completed by 1852.

B1 No. 61121 North of Potters Bar, 1949 – T. H. Watts.

Initial operations were very successful, building a positive reputation and becoming the first line to bring coal to London – slashing prices and creating a key revenue source alongside passengers and agriculture. Intentions extended beyond GNR metals though, with regular expresses to Scotland from 1862. This meant London-Edinburgh passengers now had a choice between the GNR and LNWR, and the GNR's other northern links through the NER further threatened the LNWR's erstwhile monopoly. Serious competition erupted leading to an LNWR-led 'confederacy' of disaffected companies including the York-centric MR, 'Lancashire & Yorkshire Railway' and the 'Manchester, Sheffield & Lincolnshire Railway'. A rates war developed in 1856, forcing GNR fares down to meet the 'confederacy', although ironically this boosted revenue as passengers turned to the better East Coast Main Line (ECML) service. Other features aided services, notably Britain's first dining car in 1879, by when GNR expresses were more frequent than its competitors. The GNR even provided a private saloon and engine (likely actually on standby in case of breakdowns) c.1885-1902 for Hatfield's Lord Salisbury as PM. This rivalry would peak with the ECML vs WCML 'Race to the North' of 1888 and 1895. Unofficial speed trials aiming to prove the fastest express service to Edinburgh and later Aberdeen, the lines were evenly matched averaging over 60mph. Competition would also affect GNR development and finances, supporting many branch railways to proactively expand territory and thus traffic. Funds

A4 Sparrowhawk *at Biggleswade, 1961 – B. Brooksbank*.*

The 'Flying Scotchman' service publicised in an Edwardian postcard – Author's Collection.

came from revenue rather than capital, so despite its size the company frequently risked being overstretched. At its height the GNR network covered much of the east Midlands, including Lincolnshire, Nottinghamshire and Yorkshire.

As traffic expanded, a key issue was found in south Hertfordshire. Track quadrupling, while considered from the early 1860s, was hampered by geographic constraints. Authorised in 1882 much was completed by c.1895, but remaining double-track sections at Welwyn and south of Potters Bar were problematic bottlenecks. Weakened by the 1880s through its expansionist policy, plus later WWI economies, the GNR nonetheless remained a formidable power and became the mainstay of the post-Grouping LNER.

♦ *The Route*

Running 173 miles from Kings Cross to York, c.60 miles cut north through central Hertfordshire and eastern Bedfordshire. Gradients were not severe, undulating around 1 in 200, but major civil engineering was required in places, particularly at Welwyn with two tunnels and the 40-arch Digswell Viaduct. Heading north, Hertfordshire stations served Barnet (renamed 'New Barnet' 1884; part of Hertfordshire until 1965), Hadley Wood (1885; also previously in Hertfordshire), Potters Bar (renamed 'Potter's Bar & South Mimms' 1923-71; in Herfordshire from 1965), Brookmans Park (1926), Welham Green (1986), Hatfield, Welwyn Garden City (1926; site of the 1858-60 'Welwyn Junction' and a 1920 halt, p.79), Welwyn North ('Welwyn' 1850-1926), Knebworth (1884), Stevenage, and Hitchin. Continuing into Bedfordshire were Arlesey Siding (1866, shortly renamed 'Three Counties' after a nearby asylum; closed 1959), Arlsey & Shefford Road (Arlesey spelling changed 1860, renamed 'Arlesey' 1893-5, 'Arlesey &

Henlow' 1933, closed 1959 and reopened 1988 as 'Arlesey'), Biggleswade, Sandy and Tempsford (1863, closed to passengers 1956, outright 1965).

♦ *The Hertford Loop*

Congestion grew with traffic, the Digswell Viaduct becoming an ever-tighter constraint. Rather than widen it a 24-mile bypass loop was devised running from Wood Green (London) to Stevenage (Hertfordshire), its Act passed in 1898. The first part constructed was initially a separate entity, the 1871 'Enfield Branch Railway', extension work for the loop commencing in 1905. Cuffley was reached by April 1910 but the final Stevenage leg was significantly delayed, requiring several viaducts and two tunnels while WWI limited materials available. Opened to goods on 4 March 1918 this portion was single track, itself causing traffic delays. Double track was completed in 1920 and the loop finally opened to passengers on 2 June 1924 under the LNER. Stations heading south were at Watton-at-Stone (closed 1939, reopened 1982), Stapleford (closed 1939), Hertford North, Bayford and Cuffley (1910, originally 'Cuffley & Goff's Oak'), plus seven within Greater London. Services were varied, from main-line diversions to local London-Hertford suburban trains, but the most unusual was a 1920s Hertford-Hitchin railmotor. This used Ivatt 'Motor Coaches' (a one-piece coach and tank engine) until 1924, followed by Claydon and later Sentinel steam railcars. Today it remains an important commuter route as part of the Moorgate-Finsbury Park-Hertfordshire 'Northern City Line'.

Stapleford Station on the 'Hertford Loop', 1953 – Lamberhurst Collection.*

♦ *Soviets and Stunts*

Cuffley Station welcomed many trippers viewing the downed airship *SL11* in 1916, but Brookmans Park Station would receive very different wartime visitors. On 21 May 1942 a special train pulled by A4 No. 4495 *Golden Fleece* carried a Russian delegation bound for Chequers and a secret meeting with Winston Churchill. Headed by Soviet Foreign Minister Vyacheslav Molotov, disembarking at Brookmans Park he met Anthony Eden (his British equivalent) before continuing together by road. The meeting concluded with subsequent signing of the Anglo-Soviet Treaty, confirming their military and political alliance throughout and beyond the War. Ponsbourne Tunnel (Cuffley) was the last built using traditional methods, and during WWII saw use as an emergency air-raid shelter for the Royal Train.

Arguably the best-known WCML event in modern times is the tragic Hatfield Rail Disaster of 17 October 2000, in which a fatigue-weakened rail broke resulting in four fatalities and 70 injured. The area around Hatfield has een unlucky with accidents, suffering 23 separate incidents since 1850 (albeit nany minor), six causing fatalities. One on 23 April 1860 was also caused by a roken rail (with two fatalities and 9 injured), while others of 1850, 1939 and 1968 were speed-caused collisions (collectively causing four fatalities and 60 njured). The worst, however, occurred on 26 December 1870 when a carriage vheel tyre fractured causing the train to derail. Striking a retaining wall several arriages broke up, but an oncoming coal train fortunately stopped after making nly slight contact. Sadly there were eight fatalities and three injured. Just as lestructive, rail delivery of a secret weapon to Hatfield House for testing in 1916 ielped create a military icon: as a cover against prying eyes the boxy vehicle vas called a 'tank'...

Calamity would continue at Watton-at-Stone, of a more theatrical nature. In 1977 a 'British Transport Films' production used the temporarily-closed 'Hertford Loop' for a safety film titled *The Finishing Line*. Intending to dissuade children rom playing on railway lines, it aroused controversy though the use of shock actics, graphic injuries and copious quantities of fake blood... More wholesome, hough ironically infinitely more dangerous, was the 'Hertford Loop's use in the 1929 film *The Flying Scotsman*. One of Britain's first 'talkies', the first acting role of Ray Milland and starring No. 4472 *Flying Scotsman*, its main claim to fame vere the hazardous stunts genuinely performed by the cast – including actress Pauline Johnson edging along the outside of carriages at speed in high heels! The fictional depiction was such a concern to the LNER that purportedly the pening notice highlighting real-life safety equipment was insisted on by Sir Nigel Gresley.

♦ *To BR and Beyond*

The ECML continued to be a primary route to Scotland and the north, especially goods, although revenue was hit by the Depression. Past rivalries continued against the LMS, especially through the Scottish express. Keen to promote it the service's Victorian nickname was made official in 1924: the *Flying Scotsman*. Passing to BR's Eastern Region on nationalisation, the double-track line from Hadley Wood to Potters Bar was quadrupled in 1959, new tunnels being bored

Gresley A3 Flying Scotsman, *named after the illustrious express service – Author, with permission from the Nene Valley Railway.*

while services were diverted via Hertford. Dieselisation followed, steam ceasing in 1963, with speed-boosting track upgrades by 1977. Electrification had been intended since the 1930s but delays meant work only began after the WCML. The first stage, Kings Cross to Hitchin (plus the 'Hertford Loop') was finished in 1978, the next through Bedfordshire to Huntingdon (Cambridgeshire) by 1986. Edinburgh was reached in 1991, traffic increasing substantially.

Privatisation saw several franchise holders, with suburban services (main line and 'Hertford Loop') named the *Great Northern* under 'Govia Thameslink' from 2014. In 2013 a junction flyover opened at Hitchin for the Royston-Cambridge line (p.93), leaving Welwyn as the last remaining bottleneck. Most recently in June 2018 it returned to government control with the new company 'London North Eastern Railway', echoing its historic predecessor. With many future plans the ECML will undoubtedly continue in its national importance.

The Midland Railway

Unlike other main lines, this railway was already well established before reaching London. Closely tied to other companies but developing very differently, its progressive expansion created two lines with divergent fates. Although early attempts would fade away, the final Bedford-St Pancras 'Bed-Pan' line would become the Chiltern's third northern artery.

♦ *Competitive Expansion – To Bedford and Hitchin*

The 'Midland Railway' (MR) first began under the wing of George Hudson encouraging the 1844 merger of three provincial companies. At its height it spanned much of the West Midlands, radiating from Derby to Birmingham, Sheffield and as far as Carlisle. Faced with rising competition, notably the GNR, London access was a long-standing necessity: in 1840 the constituent 'Midland Counties Railway' met the LNWR at Rugby, the MR thereafter sharing metals to Euston. Beholden to the LNWR, their trains were increasingly delayed as congestion mounted, being treated as secondary to the LNWR's own. Despit amalgamation talks relations ever-deteriorated until the MR changed sides, turning to the GNR. A Hudson-proposed Leicester-Hitchin line had previously been authorised in 1847 (amid considerable GNR opposition) but was abandone due to the national post-'Mania' depression. Urged on by locals and the prospect of Northamptonshire iron ore traffic, a new Act in 1853 was passed – GNR opposition withdrawn after agreeing a connecting service.

Construction fell to engineer Charles Liddell and contractor Thomas Brassey but the ongoing Crimean War dissuaded investors and increased costs. Furthe delays occurred, land valuation issues moving the Hitchin junction north with 3 miles of parallel running, while LNWR discussions for a joint station at Bedford collapsed (despite later Mayoral pressure), delaying construction. After a Director's special and feast, coal trains began on 15 April 1857 followed by goods (4 May) and passengers on 8 May, temporarily using Bedford LNWR Station via a spur. However, the GNR insisted on trains terminating at Hitchin, passengers to purchase tickets and continue via GNR services. Through trains only began on 1 February 1858 after a seven-year arrangement with a guaranteed £20,000 minimum annual toll.

Going Alone – On to St Pancras

The line was a boon for the MR, opening potential to GNR-connected locations and with growing passenger and mineral traffic, but company unity did not last. Hitchin Station was problematic – trains had to cross ECML running lines to reach the platform and reverse out while working around GNR services. Congestion mounted, MR trains increasingly delayed in favour of the GNR's, worsened by the ECML's double track capacity – a MR train being involved in the 1866 Welwyn Tunnel accident. Tensions finally boiled over with excursion traffic in 1862. As the MR was completing its own London coal depot the GNR (needing carriage space) withdrew access to its Kings Cross sidings. Frustrated, the MR requested permanent future running powers, the GNR refusing but offering to quadruple its line – in return for tripling the annual toll. The MR unsurprisingly rejected this and in 1863 an Act was granted for its own line to St Pancras. GNR opposition had failed, especially as the LNWR withdrew theirs, the new line enacting poetic revenge by encroaching on several GNR branches and ultimately taking over the London coal trade. Contractual use of Kings Cross continued until 1870, some MR trains also still using the LNWR.

Built by Liddell and Brassey (although arguably more Brassey's partner Stephen Ballard), goods commenced on 9 September 1867 but delays meant passenger services only began on 13 July 1868. Using Moorgate MET Station (expresses still to Kings Cross), St Pancras itself was only finally opened on 1 October. Passenger traffic was initially slow, hampered by national recession, but grew substantially by the 1880s with commuting and wider MR expansion. New provisions were equally introduced, notably 1874 Pullman cars, and in 1875 being the first company to abolish second class. Goods likewise blossomed, Bedford in particular benefitting with new industries including 'W.H. Allen & Son' (builders of dynamos for the *Titanic*) and 'Simplex', whose narrow gauge locomotives would be prevalent during WWI. The substantial private siding to Napsbury hospital (1905) was similarly important during the War.

Growing traffic pressured capacity, so a third goods-only track south was built at Luton in 1875. This became the first of many sporadic additions, each followed separately by a fourth northbound track. These sections were joined up c.1895, quadrupling the route, although only becoming passenger 'slow' lines in 1906. Of particular note were the 'Bedford Curve' enabling fast trains to bypass the station and at Sharnbrook where the new goods-only tracks used a tunnel and the gradient-reducing 'Wymington Deviation'. By the Grouping the *Midland Main Line* (MML) was not only nationally important but St Pancras the centrepiece of the LMS.

Meanwhile, the Bedford-Hitchin line had lost its main line rank. Not designed for intermediate traffic, it began a simple branch shuttle service with occasional through mineral trains. A siding for London refuse opened in 1893 but in 1911 the double track was singled, all bar Shefford to Southill – saved by local farmers.

'Cardington Station with the looming airship sheds, 1987 – B. Brooksbank*.

Even with 1920s airship development at Cardington, culminating in the ill-fatec *R101*, interwar buses hastened its decline.

♦ *The Route*

Passing north-south for c.45 miles through central Bedfordshire anc Hertfordshire, the 99-mile MML saved money by following topography, allowin steeper gradients such as the 1 in 119 summit at Sharnbrook. Even so cutting and tunnels were required, second bores added when quadrupled. Includin those north of Bedford built for the initial Hitchin route, stations heading soutl were at Sharnbrook (closed 1960), Oakley (closed to passengers 1958, outigh 1963), Bedford (1859, 'Bedford Midland Road' 1924-78 then 'Bedford Midland to 1988), Ampthill (closed 1959), Flitwick (1870), Harlington, Leagrave, Lutor ('Luton Midland Road' until the 1950-60s), Chiltern Green ('Chiltern Green fo Luton Hoo' from 1891, closed 1952), then in Hertfordshire at Harpenden, S Albans City, Napsbury (1905, closed 1959), Radlett and Elstree (named 'Elstre & Boreham Wood' 1869-1904 and 'Elstree & Borehamwood' 1953-74 and fron 1988).

As for the relegated Hitchin line, its 15 miles ran southwest across the countie with minimal engineering to save funds – gradients rising up to 1 in 120. Th sole concession was the Warden Tunnel between Cardington and Southill. Afte Bedford stations were at Cardington, Cardington Workmen's Platform (a 1917-2 halt), Southill, Shefford and Henlow (renamed 'Henlow Camp' 1933).

♦ *Flying Along...*

Just after closure the Hitchin line gained brief celebrity during filming of th 1965 *Those Magnificent Men in their Flying Machines*. Warden Tunnel stood in fo France, Terry Thomas' plane landing on the roof of a train with unfortunat consequences... Having no air vents, suffering from smoke, the tunnel als triggered other incidents. One goods driver ran ahead of his moving train t get clean air, while another fireman climbed down the tender steps beneat he smoke – frightening the driver vho suddenly found himself alone ɔn the footplate!

Luton has been scene of several .ccidents, but one would be partly .ttributed to the well-known Vauxhall' motor factory. On :2 December 1955 a St Pancras-.eicester service was just departing vhen forced to halt by late ɔassengers trying to board. Having ɔassed the home signal, the ignalman had already accepted he following express but kept its ignals at danger. Unfortunately he lights at 'Vauxhall' helped ɔbscure the distant signal, the ·xpress driver missing it and only ɔraking with the home signal. Jnable to stop, it ploughed into he stationary train which partially telescoped, causing one fatality and 23 njured. Although the driver was primarily at fault, the lighting was rearranged .fter the accident. Speed would surface more positively on 1 July 2012, when he highest record speed was attained on the MML. Undertaking tests of train-nduced pressure waves in the Ampthill Tunnel, a Class 222 Diesel Multiple Unit DMU) attained 125mph, enabling part of the line to be authorised for faster unning.

Warden Tunnel from the air, 2016 – T. Monk.

Differing Futures

VWII brought a reprieve for the Hitchin line, RAF Cardington and Henlow eceiving troop trains and supplies (aided by their own internal railways), but t ended with Peace. Reduced to one-coach trains in the 1950s under BR, 'Park ?oyal' railbuses were trialled in 1958 (nicknamed 'Greenhouses') followed by)MUs, but services reverted to steam push-pull. The last passenger train quietly leparted on 30 December 1961, services ceasing on 1 January 1962, although final railtour visited in 1963. General goods ended on 28 December 1964; 3edford-RAF Cardington supplies the sole remaining function until final closure n 1969. Today some stations are private houses and a nature reserve surrounds Varden Tunnel, but much of the trackbed has become field borders. Reopening ıas been considered under the *Varsity Line* 'East-West Rail' project, but with lternate options available its potential future remains undecided.

As for the MML it was subject to BR's changes, from suburban and express lieselisation in 1960, famously the *Midland Pullman* service, to a Beeching-dvised passenger service modification. After Privatisation franchise operations ame under 'East Midlands Railway' in 2019 and suburban to Bedford under

'Govia Thameslink' from 2014 Electrification was mooted ir 1976 from St Pancras to Bedford completed on 28 March 1983 but extension northwards stallec until the erstwhile 2012 'Electri Spine' project. Completec through the Chilterns to Corby (Northamptonshire) in 2021 including re-quadrupling a Sharnbrook (reduced to thre tracks in 1987), the rest i yet to be finished. Amid thi modernisation a former S Albans City signalbox has conversely been preserved, a scarce example still ir situ. A vital route still advancing, for now the MML remains one of the last majo diesel main lines.

St Albans City Station, 1947 – T.H. Watts.

The Metropolitan Railway

The pioneering line of the world's first underground railway, the 'Metropolitar Railway' (MET) founded a London icon. Beyond the City, however, it also formec a main line in its own right, exclusive to the Chilterns. Divided by northerr decline versus southern prosperity, it ultimately experienced two very differen destinies.

♦ *Underground to Overground*

Authorised in 1854, a 3.5-mile line under central London addressing roac congestion, the first train of this ambitious project ran on 10 January 1863 Expansion immediately followed, opening to Swiss Cottage by 1868, but furthe plans failed. At this time the MET was wrapped in a Hudson-esque financia scandal, worsened by low passenger levels. Brought in to allay shareholder fears new Chairman Sir Edward Watkin saw a solution: new lines generating nev traffic. By 1880 extensions had brought the MET to Harrow on the Hill.

With sights on Aylesbury, finances meant the intended line would ultimatel be constructed as several smaller segments each under its own Act. Under enginee Charles Liddell, the first to Rickmansworth (Hertfordshire) was authorised in 188C trains starting on 1 September 1887. A further Act to Aylesbury was passed in 188 but capital was increasingly difficult to raise – naysayers predicting failure due t the area's sparse rural population. Instead, work turned to a branch to Cheshan (roughly halfway) authorised in 1885 – pushed by enthusiastic locals who eve donated £2,000 towards the station site. Opening without ceremony on 8 Jul 1889, double track continued only up to Chalfont, the diverging branch bein single. Thoughts of its potential continuation to the LNWR never developed. Wor from Chalfont to Aylesbury finally started in 1890, opened with a celebrator luncheon on 1 September 1892, but Watkin's expansion was not yet finished.

Rickmansworth Station's unusual curved platform, forced by reluctant landowners – P. Hodge.

• The Aylesbury & Buckingham Railway

efore all these constructions egan, attention had turned to n existing Buckinghamshire ne that, while never carrying nuch heavy traffic, would ecome an important part of 1ET development. The 1850 3uckinghamshire Railway' (p.48) ad intended a line to Aylesbury ut LNWR indifference stymied construction. Rebuffed locals including Sir Harry 'erney (a major local rail advocate) and the Marquis of Chandos still wanted he line, forming the 'Aylesbury & Buckingham Railway' (ABR) and gaining an ct in 1860. Another supporter was local up-and-coming politician Benjamin Disraeli. Running from Aylesbury to Claydon (renamed Verney Junction after ir Harry) the route changed substantially, Chandos influencing a detour to the vest of Quainton Hill closer to his Wotton estate. A connection to the Aylesbury NWR branch was intended but opposition instead led to joint use of the rival GWR-run 'Wycombe Railway' (WR) Aylesbury Station (p.60). Construction was low, hampered by financial issues, the single track opening on 23 September 868. Borrowed rolling stock had to be brought in via Oxford-Claydon, the road gauge WR only converting to standard gauge in October. Continued NWR hostility meant despite the line's name there were never any Aylesbury-

1ET No. 1 heading south from Cheshunt – P. Hodge.

Old and new: Metrovick No. 12 *Sarah Siddons* and 'S Stock' at Amersham – P. Hodge.

Buckingham services, and with local traffic barely existent the line was not a success. In 1874 the GWR considered absorbing the line but declined, it remaining privately-owned with its own staff.

Little changed over the 1880s until involvement from the MET. Invited to the ABR Board in 1875 Watkin encouraged furtherin their extension aspirations to Harrow, to meet the MET. Although authorise the plan collapsed, the MET expanding instead (under Watkin's persuasion) an purchasing the ABR, taking over from 1 July 1891. Not yet physically connecte to the MET, GWR operation continued under a new agreement. MET trains o reaching Aylesbury first used a temporary station until discussions enabled new joint one, opened on 1 January 1894. Unfortunately, the ABR's lightweigh track blocked heavy MET engines, forcing local-only services using specifically acquired D Class 2-4-0Ts (previously borrowing LNWR stock) after GWR service suddenly ended on 31 March 1894. Modified with double track and upgrade stations, commencement of through services on 1 January 1897 meant ME expansion was finally complete.

♦ *The Route*

Stretching 50 miles from Baker Street, c.35 miles ran northwest through wester Hertfordshire and central Buckinghamshire. Gradients taxed trains even wit cuttings and embankments, much of the route north of Rickmansworth throug the Chiltern Hills being around 1 in 100. The ex-ABR was flatter in the Val of Aylesbury, but similarly rose 1 in 111 to a summit at Hogshaw Bank nea

Preservation on the former ABR at Quainton – Author, with permission from the Buckinghamshire Railway Centre.

Quainton. Heading north, Hertfordshire stations served Moor Park (1910, initially 'Sandy Lodge' then 'Moor Park & Sandy Lodge' 1923-50), Rickmansworth and Chorley Wood ('Chorley Wood & Chenies' 1915-34 and 'Chorleywood' from 1965). In Buckinghamshire were Chalfont & Latimer ('Chalfont Road' until 1915), Chesham, Amersham ('Amersham & Chesham Bois' 1922-34, although after reverting back the signs were unchanged until 1948!), Great Missenden, Wendover, Stoke Mandeville and Aylesbury (1863, 'Aylesbury Town' 1950-63). Continuing on the ex-ABR were Waddesdon Manor (1897, 'Waddesdon' from 1922), Quainton Road, Grandborough Road ('Granborough' spelling changed 1920), Winslow Road and Verney Junction.

◆ *Provinces and Preservation*

A side enterprise of the MET created a Chiltern icon: 'Metro-Land'. Promoting rural living with easy commuting, 'Metropolitan Railway Country Estates Ltd' was founded in 1919 creating complete housing estates around the railway. Massively successful, it became the benchmark for British suburbs. Used as a backdrop for several episodes of *The Avengers*, Metroland reached its cultural pinnacle with John Betjeman's poetry and 1973 documentary of life along the line. It failed to develop at its northernmost, however, Betjeman declaring of Verney Junction that *'grass triumphs, and I must say, I'm rather glad'*. Aside from suburbs Rickmansworth would also hold an unusual record. The 1925-61 terminus of electrification, engines were switched from electric to steam to continue north. The process took barely three minutes and was claimed to be the fastest changeover in the world.

Following the 1989 centenary of Chesham Station the line regularly hosted heritage stock at annual 'Steam on the MET' events until 2000, guest engines operating specials between ordinary services. Steam returned in 2013 for the MET's 150th anniversary, but part of the ABR retains active preservation. Formed in 1962 the 'London Railway Preservation Society' acquired numerous vehicles, initially stored at Luton and Bishop's Stortford. Seeking a permanent base, in 1971 the 'Quainton Railway Society' was founded, creating the 'Buckinghamshire Railway Centre'. Now an accredited museum it features numerous historic buildings, working rolling stock and displays, and has been a frequent filming location, from *Midsomer Murders* to *Doctor Who*.

◆ *Countryside Commutes*

Things barely settled before a significant change – connection to the 'Great Central Railway' (GCR). Sharing tracks (later joint managed), their turbulent relationship nonetheless aided traffic. Goods only began in 1880 but grew rapidly along the extension (a key factor behind its construction), boosted by northern GCR connections. Aylesbury milk was especially notable alongside building supplies to London housing developments, in turn requiring rail-fed supplies. Passenger traffic similarly grew with ever-more season tickets, aided by additional services including 1910 Pullmans (competing with the GCR) and 1908 inter-company marketing as the 'Underground'. Also MGCJR joint-

Winslow Road Station (ex-ABR) – Lamberhurst Collection.*

operated, ex-ABR services included short-lived 1905-14 GCR railmotors and push-pull Aylesbury trains from 1906. In 1905 electrification reached Harrow but its continuation was stopped by WWI. Wartime traffic was major – over 26,000 military trains – plus a 1917 spur to RFC Halton at Wendover (later RAF; closed 1963). Cementing its main line status passenger traffic rose further, and on 5 January 1925 electrification reached Rickmansworth, the heart of Metroland.

Exempt from the 1923 Grouping, on 1 July 1933 the MET became part of the 'London Passenger Transport Board' (LPBT), branded as *London Transport*. The fiercely-independent MET had heavily opposed formation of this public corporation, but as bus competition and the Depression saw falling passenger traffic it instead looked to compensation. Becoming the *Metropolitan Line*, at its 1930s' height the former MET spanned not only the Chilterns but parts of several subsequent underground lines.

Focussing on central London the first LPBT change was ending goods services, transferred to the LNER (ex-GCR) on 1 November 1937. The main line itself equally jarred with this inner-city image and MET services north of Aylesbury were withdrawn on 6 July 1936. Quainton briefly resumed MET passenger duties c.1943-8, however, likely with war traffic including to an adjoining food store. Deemed unviable, bypassed by the GCR and without suburban development the upper ex-ABR simultaneously closed to passengers (both MET and LNER), the last train passing on 4 July. Through goods traffic continued but declined with the 1940 GCR-*Varsity* spur. Singled north of Quainton by 1940, this closed outright on 8 September 1947 after a final railtour. Part remained as a siding until 1961; little remains today, although Granborough Road Station was referenced in the 2012 Bond film *Skyfall*.

The LPBT was nationalised alongside BR in 1948, renamed the 'London Transport Executive'. Modernisation was central and electrification – part of the ex-LPTB's 'New Works' programme delayed by WWII – was completed to Amersham on 14 August 1960 and Chesham on 12 September. MET passenger steam (supplied by the LNER/BR) ceased on 9 September 1961. The next day Amersham became the northernmost MET terminus, Aylesbury Underground services ending and the track transferring to BR. Interwar quadrupling plans were also completed, reaching the Watford branch junction (p.139) on 17 June 1962. By then passenger numbers had declined, only recovering with 1980s' Travelcards, but unlike with Beeching MET services were unchanged. The BTC's abolition triggered new management, passing through several bodies until the public-private partnership 'Transport for London' (TFL) took control on 15 July 2003. Organising future upgrades while recognising its history, the MET and its former main line remains a key Chiltern connection.

The Great Central Railway

Britain's last steam-era main line, its tumultuous history is reflected in Buckinghamshire's criss-crossed tracks. Involved with the MET and GWR, rurality and hostility hampered its consolidation, becoming arguably Beeching's greatest single victim. Surviving portions nonetheless continue to have a valuable role.

♦ *Grand Plans*

In 1847 three companies merged to form the 'Manchester, Sheffield & Lincolnshire Railway', a provincial line stretching at its height from Liverpool to Grimsby (much through joint lines). Not overly successful, its primary traffic was coal but London-bound it depended on other railways – LNWR enmity leading to GNR cooperation. In 1854 Edward Watkin became Manager, then Chairman in 1864. Ultimately chairman of nine separate railways, he envisioned these uniting into a grand line from Lancashire to the south coast. Key to this, also boosting profits while reducing external dependency, was a GCR London link. Attempts to encourage other companies (notably the MET) to merge or build northwards failed, triggering its own southbound construction – reaching Annesley (Nottinghamshire) in 1893. Claims of aiming for Paris via his Channel Tunnel appear unfounded; it was equally not built to Continental loading gauge.

Although defeated in 1892 (opposition including from the GNR for breaking a traffic agreement), a London Extension Act was granted in 1893. Running from Annesley to Quainton Road, Watkin as Chairman of both companies arranged shared use of the MET, but after his 1894 retirement through ill health the intended joint-use of Baker Street changed to a bespoke terminus at Marylebone. Split between contractors, construction under engineer Sir Douglas Fox began in 1894, but underestimated costs meant funds remained tight even with MET investment. Reflecting its ambitions, on 1 August 1897 the company was renamed, becoming the 'Great Central Railway' (GCR).

Commencing coal trains on 25 July 1898, it was ceremonially opened on 9 March 1899 before passenger services from 15 March. Goods following on

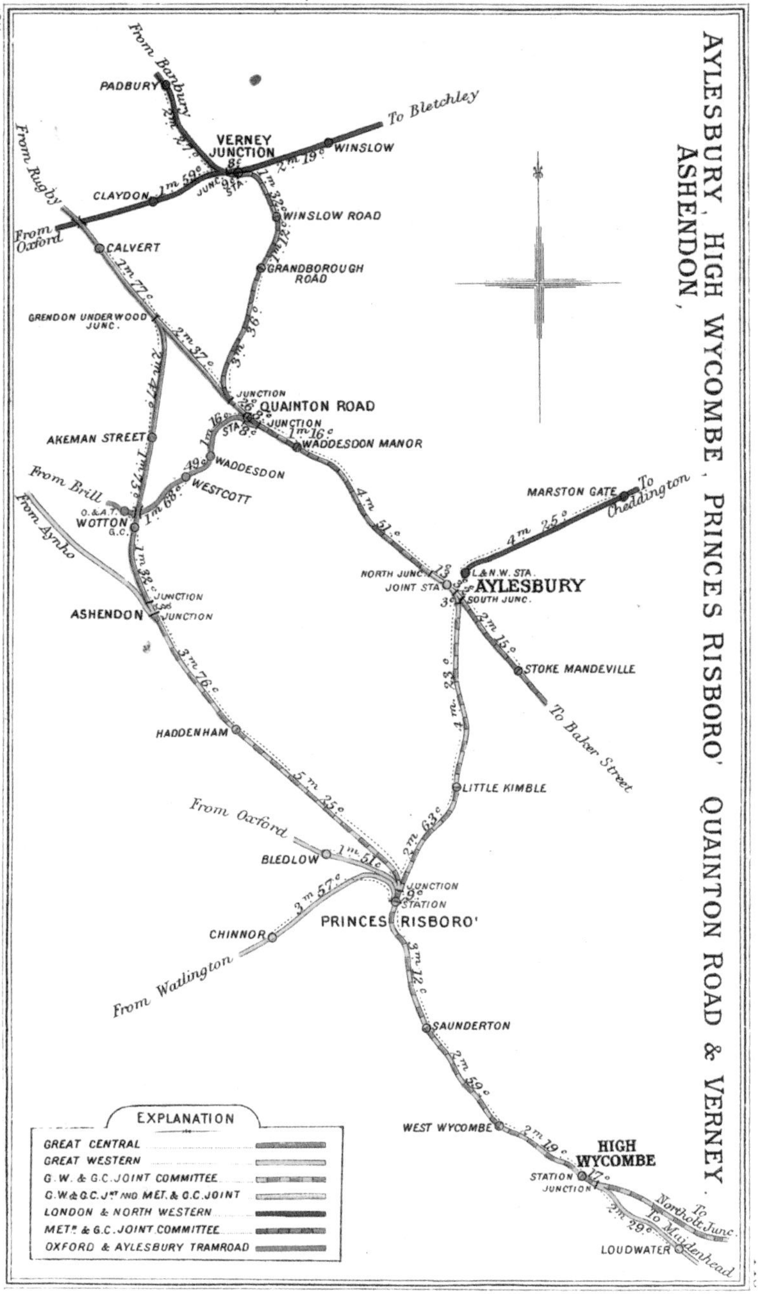

The railways of northern Buckinghamshire, 1914 – Railway Clearing House.*

Akeman Street Station, c.1900 – Lamberhurst Collection.*

11 April, coal a particularly key traffic, but there were immediate problems. Concerns about the line's viability came true: built too late, as a rural through route serving already-connected locations the predicted traffic growth never occurred. Competing with other long-established routes passenger numbers was especially sluggish – the first Marylebone train contained only four people. These prevented issuing any dividend, disillusioned shareholders redefining 'GCR' as 'Gone Completely'. Furthermore, Watkin's joint lines rarely included actual cooperation, his retirement coupled with personal animosity between Managers John Bell (MET) and Harry Pollitt (GCR) causing all unity to collapse. Fortunately traffic improved by the 1900s, albeit primarily goods and still lesser than its rivals, the GCR building a reputation for fast punctual services promoted as 'Rapid Travel in Luxury'.

♦ *A Necessary Alternative*

MET difficulties became such a hindrance that the GCR turned elsewhere. The GWR, having already collaborated over a GCR link to Banbury, wished to shorten their Oxford-Birmingham route (struggling against the shorter WCML), so united to build a new line: the 'Great Western & Great Central Joint Railway' (GWGCJR). Authorised in 1899 under

Quainton Road Station – Author, with permission from the Buckinghamshire Railway Centre.

engineer James Inglis, protracted construction with over-running costs meant the so-named 'Alternate Route' only commenced goods running on 20 November 1905; through passenger services from 2 April 1906. Unusually the opening luncheon was hosted by High Wycombe for the Directors, rather than vice versa. Its effect was immediate: although 5 miles longer than the MET, faster services with improved capacity (no longer blocked by MET stopping trains) encouraged passengers – Marylebone traffic doubling. While becoming a notable through route, especially goods, local traffic conversely was limited. Despite promoting local market trains suburban expansion was slower than hoped (even with additional stations, only increasing after WWI), local goods similarly lacking. With these traffic issues, despite two London links the GCR ultimately never realised its ambitions, remaining secondary to other routes north.

Robinson 9P No. 1165 Valour *near Harrow, c.1910 – Grace's Guide to British Industrial History.*

As for the bypassed MET, the potential loss of GCR revenue (plus its own construction outlay) led to a revised agreement, aided by a change in managers. Authorised in 1905 – before the GWGCJR was even complete – it leased track, guaranteed traffic (£45,000 worth annually), and most significantly from 2 April 1906 created the 'Metropolitan & Great Central Joint Railway' (MGCJR). Controlling daily operations, management and maintenance alternated between the companies every five years until 1926, when permanently set to reduce wastefulness.

♦ *The Route*

The 92-mile double-track GCR extension was built learning from its predecessors, with wide curves and a maximum 1 in 176 gradient to aid high speeds. These stipulations made cutting through the Chiltern Hills more challenging; earthworks and viaducts being additional costs. Entering north Buckinghamshire the GCR only traversed 7 miles before reaching the MET at Quainton Road Junction. Of the nine stations south of Rugby only Calvert was in Buckinghamshire, named after Sir Harry Verney. Finmere (Oxfordshire) was also initially named as being 'for Buckingham'. While built to the latest standards the MET conversely was not – one of many issues between the two companies. With tighter curves, heavier gradients and shorter blocks between signalboxes long goods trains had to be split, a yard being constructed at Quainton. Sharing MET stations (p.33), now also serving Aylesbury Vale Parkway (2008), the GCR branched towards Marylebone beyond Hertfordshire at Harrow on the Hill.

Between Calvert and Quainton, Grendon Underwood Junction led south to the GWGCJR. Running to Ashendon, this 5.5-mile link track was primarily a through route, but little-used stations opened at Akeman Street (closed to passengers

1930, outright 1931) and Wotton (closed 1953). Continuing south the GWGCJR ran southwest loosely parallel to the MET for 34 miles, diverging at Northolt for Paddington and Marylebone (via Neasden). Central to this was appropriation and upgrading of part of the ex-WR. Topography again led to major civil engineering for low gradients, especially viaducts. In particular, the WR's Saunderton Bank was a 1 in 88 gradient; thought too steep for coal trains, it was modified including a separate southbound loop with cuttings and tunnel. Stations heading south were at Haddenham & Thame Parkway (1987), Haddenham, Ilmer Halt (1929), then four ex-WR stations at Princes Risborough, Saunderton, West Wycombe and High Wycombe (p.62) before Beaconsfield, Seer Green (1915, 'Beaconsfield Golf Links Halt' until 1918 and 'Seer Green & Jordans' 1950-74), Gerrards Cross (initially 'Gerrards Cross for the Chalfonts'), Denham Golf Club (1912, initially 'Denham Golf Club Platform') and Denham (originally 'Denham – Junction for Uxbridge'; p.138). Double-tracked, many stations had loops (removed under BR) enabling through services to overtake stopped local trains.

♦ *The Last Main Line?*

While the GCR is considered Britain's final steam-era main line there was technically one more – the last built before the 2003 'Channel Tunnel Rail Link'. Authorised in 1905, opened 4 April 1910 to goods and 1 July for passengers, the GWR *Bicester Cut-Off* ran northwest from the GWGCJR Ashendon Junction through Bicester to Aynho Junction (Northamptonshire) on the GWR Oxford-Birmingham line. This 18-mile link completed the GWR's shortened northbound route, bypassing Oxford and becoming their primary route north. The previously-joint Ashendon-Grendon Underwood link subsequently became GCR-only. Having six stations, those in Buckinghamshire were Brill & Ludgershall and Dorton Halt (1937) – the latter opened in response to the poor position of the former plus the closure of the nearby Brill branch (p.119). This line encountered similar topography issues to the GCR, its civil engineering including the Brill Tunnel. Focussing on through passenger traffic, demand led to ever-farther destinations, notably the 1927 *Cambrian Coast Express* to Wales. Local auto-trains also operated, while Bicester ultimately had Britain's final slip coach service, ceasing in 1960.

♦ *Tracks and Tribulations*

Animosity between the GCR and MET ever-increased, but it was already marked even before the GCR opened. Prevaricating over timetabling initial coal trains (intended to bed the track in), GCR Manager Pollitt successfully pushed for test trains. However, the first commercial coal train arrived at 3:00am – before the agreed start time. MET Manager Bell personally went to Quainton, overseeing the signalman and blocking its access to MET metals. Preventing the engine from even running round the train (it being dangerous to propel backwards), disruption ensued until another engine came to take it away. The next day trains began in earnest, but things hardly improved afterwards: in 1901 a furious King Edward VII's GCR Royal Train was ten minutes late, being – by accident or design – placed behind a MET slow goods!

A new supermarket in Gerrards Cross led to a tunnel being constructed over a cutting in 2005. On 30 June, still incomplete, it collapsed blocking both lines. No-one was injured but a train about to enter had to make an emergency stop; other trains were duly halted. It took two months to clear the line, and a replacement tunnel was completed in 2010.

Aylesbury was also scene of a major accident. When the MET first reached the station the junction included a sharp curve, limited to 15mph which caused difficulties with later fast through-running. Early on 23 December 1904 a northbound GCR newspaper express passing through heavy fog hit the curve at 60mph and derailed. The engine and 3-4 leading vehicles mounted the 'down' platform, two on the 'up' platform and the rest disintegrated, spread over 50 yards. As essentially a fast goods those aboard were all railway staff, with four fatalities. A London-bound express then ran into the wreckage, fortunately without injury. Officially the cause was excessive speed, questionable familiarity with the route and an insufficient length of check rail on the points, but competitive pressure on the GCR to make newspaper runs as quickly as possible undoubtedly added to the disaster. In 1908 the station was rebuilt and the junction realigned. In the immediate aftermath many locals helped clear debris – especially the contents of a destroyed van filled with Christmas puddings...

♦ *Decline and Resurgence*

With the Grouping the GCR came under the LNER, the two joint lines continuing as before. The first substantial change was to the MGCJR with 1936 LPTB reductions: Underground trains terminating at Aylesbury (later Amersham) and the northern remainder solely under LNER operation. LNER expresses increasingly used the MGCJR, those on the GWGCJR mostly GWR-run. Still

The 1904 Aylesbury Disaster – Author's Collection.

Jubilee No. 5690 Leander *at Seer Green Station – O. Chapman.*

'Give Peas a Chance!': the Chalfont Viaduct – S. Ballard.*

secondary to other main lines ex-GCR goods nonetheless grew, especially during WWII with several local RAF bases.

Joint line management finally disappeared under Nationalisation, being divided between the main operators – Underground, Eastern (MGCJR) and Western (GWGCJR) Regions. Initially successful with named trains such as the *Master Cutler,* in 1958 the ex-GCR main line was transferred from Eastern to London Midland Region. Historic rivals, it was seen as duplicating the MML and services began to be transferred, the line increasingly neglected. 1960s dieselisation did little to help, decreasing goods (especially coal) and rising car usage hampering it further. Ex-GCR through expresses ended on 2 January 1960, Aynho line locals on 7 January 1963 and local services north of Princes Risborough/Aylesbury on 4 March 1963 – Brill & Ludgershall, Dorton Halt, Haddenham and Ilmer Halt closing outright. Calvert and Quainton Road briefly became goods-only before similarly closing. Only semi-fast London-Nottingham services remained, and with BR claiming a *'deteriorating financial position'* amid allegations of being deliberately run-down for potential closure, the GCR's place in the Beeching Report was sealed.

On 3 September 1966 the last train ran between Aylesbury and Rugby, closing as a through route despite public protest on 5 September – Beeching's biggest cut. Other withdrawals ensured the GCR's final closure in 1969. Track north of Calvert was lifted in 1968, the Aylesbury-Calvert MGCJR being singled for goods-only use – remaining passenger trains terminating at Aylesbury. Barely used after the end of 1960 expresses (northbound GCR passenger trains thereafter using the MGCJR) and essentially singled following a goods derailment in 1965, the GWGCJR Ashendon link similarly closed, although only officially on 21 July 1967. Part remained as a private siding until c.1989. GWGCJR commuter trains

The opening of Haddenham & Thame Parkway Station, 3 October 1987 – Lamberhurst Collection.*

thereafter terminated at Princes Risborough/Aylesbury, the line to Banbury transferring from Western to London Midland Region on 24 March 1974. The Aynho line saw increased use during WCML electrification but on 5 March 1967 through services ceased, the line downgraded and singled north of Princes Risborough in 1968 with just Marylebone-Banbury DMUs running by 1974.

Even with poor services 1980s commuter traffic was marked – Quainton briefly reopening for occasional shopping specials. Christened the *Chiltern Line* by 'Network SouthEast' in 1985, closure of Marylebone was considered in 1986 but rejected in favour of modernisation. This was completed by 1992, including higher MGCJR speeds and the new 1987 GWGCJR Haddenham & Thame Parkway Station. Passenger traffic grew, reinvigorating the lines until in 1993 the GWGCJR even regained London-Birmingham services (now from Marylebone). Operated by 'Chiltern Railways' after Privatisation further work followed, notably re-doubling Princes Risborough-Bicester in 1998 and opening Aylesbury Vale Parkway Station on 14 December 2008, extending ex-MGCJR passenger services northwards. Still serving Aylesbury, Princes Risborough and through to Birmingham, today little remained of the closed parts, just borders between fields, but north of Aylesbury remained active with Calvert 'Binliner' rubbish trains until lifted in 2021. Plans existed for partial reopening up to the *Varsity Line* with more upgrades, however, further GCR reopening appears overtaken by the nearby *High Speed 2*. Stronger than ever before, the *Chiltern Line* presents an apt successor for the past ambitions of the GCR.

GCR-designed O4 No. 3043 at Seer Green, 1950 – B. Brooksbank.*

II: Regional lines

Regional Lines of the Chilterns

Lines and operating companies at their height, 1925

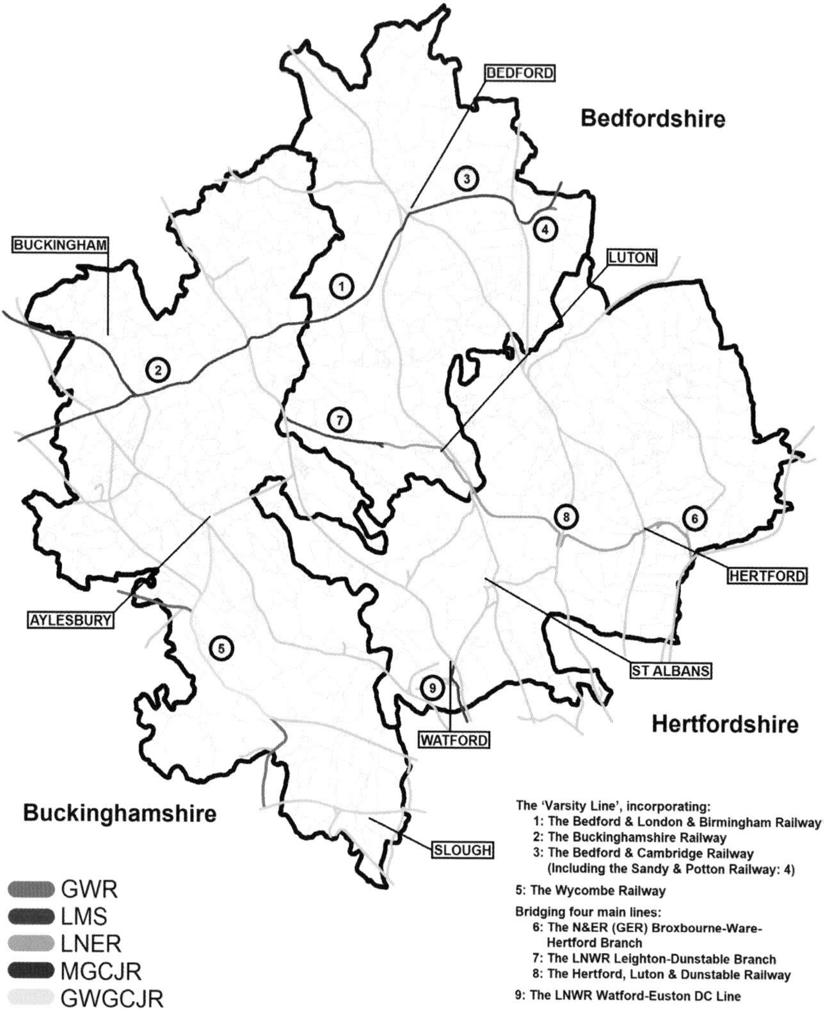

The 'Varsity Line', incorporating:
1: The Bedford & London & Birmingham Railway
2: The Buckinghamshire Railway
3: The Bedford & Cambridge Railway
(Including the Sandy & Potton Railway: 4)

5: The Wycombe Railway

Bridging four main lines:
6: The N&ER (GER) Broxbourne-Ware-Hertford Branch
7: The LNWR Leighton-Dunstable Branch
8: The Hertford, Luton & Dunstable Railway

9: The LNWR Watford-Euston DC Line

Main lines have obvious national importance but there were other equally vital cross-county railways. From an area's sole connection to key commuter routes, each helped underpin local economies and town prestige. Britain's railway development also led to a problem that itself elevated the importance of certain tracks. Most major companies focussed on London, main lines running from north to south. The few west-east lines consequently gained value, enabling regions to be crossed internally without resorting to a London detour. Sadly, failure to recognise this use in the 1960s means few remain today – a blow for public transport accessibility.

Many major stations had motive power depots, Bletchley's serving several local branches (shown in 1955) – Lamberhurst Collection.*

Crossing the Chilterns: The Varsity Line

Stretching at its height from Oxford to Cambridge, the five railways that formed the Oxbridge *Varsity Line* and its Buckingham branch created a west-east route of national importance. Connecting six major lines (GWR, GCR, LNWR, MR, GNR and GER), traffic could transfer between them from across the country without entering the ever-more congested London alongside serving local populations and businesses. Later mothballed despite its value, new plans offer a vibrant future.

♦ *From Bletchley to Bedford*

The launch of the London & Birmingham Railway (LBR), opened great traffic potential from Bedfordshire to Linslade Station, but road limitations were a major problem. By the 1840s Hertford and Cambridge had gained rail connections and,

Woburn Sands Station, c.1880 – Author's Collection.

recognising the benefits, Bedford was keen to do likewise. Following a failed 1836 proposal a public meeting was held on 23 April 1844 attended by George Stephenson. The 'Bedford Railway' was subsequently formed, George and son Robert the line's engineers. Importantly, unlike early lines elsewhere it had support from the local gentry, including the Duke of Bedford. An Act for the 'Bedford & London & Birmingham Railway' was passed in 1845 and the LBR agreed to operate it via a junction at Bletchley. The first sod was cut by the Duchess of Bedford on 13 December 1845 and under 'Grissel, Peto & Jackson' construction was swift, if occasionally hindered. Land was expensive – one Thomas Bennett sold at the excessive sum of £1,000 per acre. The line was ready for opening by October 1846, running powers under the newly-formed LNWR, but this was delayed as severe rain triggered subsidence. On 17 November the first train departed amid celebration with 600 passengers. Met by the Duchess on its return, a champagne party was followed by dinner at Bedford Assembly Rooms.

Opened to the public the next day, its impact was marked. Charging half the price of road travel for double the speed, stagecoaches declined (replaced by growing station-supporting omnibuses), while coal prices fell sharply. The Duke's estate gained substantially from timber export, and Bletchley started growing into an important location with five Bedford trains daily. The company had been primarily focused on construction alone, and immediately after opening the LNWR as majority share-holders purchased the line, although the former company was only officially dissolved on 21 July 1879. Operation would quietly continue until 1862 and a new connection.

♦ *To Banbury and Oxford*

Meanwhile other schemes were developing. Lying between the LBR and GWR, cross-fighting led to various proposals encircling northern Buckinghamshire, notably the GWR Oxford-Rugby line via Banbury (later to Birmingham) which the LBR was keen to prevent expanding into the county. Buckingham itself had been overlooked and local figures similarly sought a connection, notably the Marquis of Chandos and Sir Harry Verney, forming the 'Buckingham & Brackley

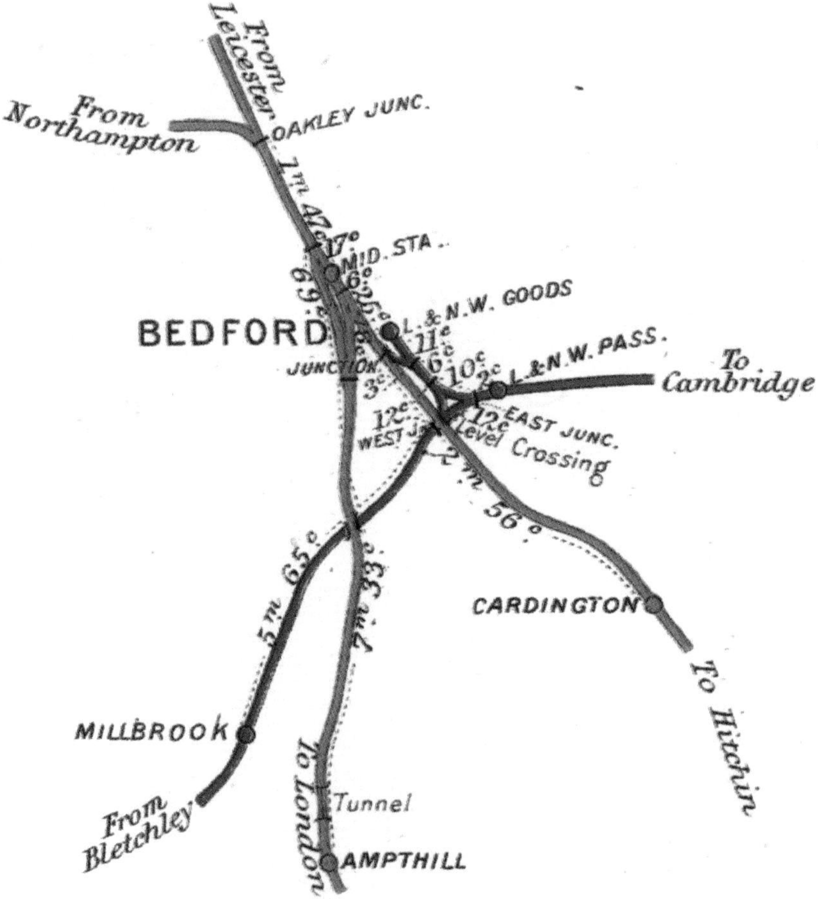

The railways of Bedford, 1914 – Railway Clearing House.*

Junction Railway'. Simultaneously the 'Oxford & Bletchley Junction Railway' was promoted (with Verney as Chairman) forming a link with the GWR's Oxford line. These two companies collectively planned a cross, comprising Bletchley to Oxford via Bicester (west-east) plus Buckingham via Brackley down to Aylesbury (north-south). The meeting point of these would be near Middle Claydon. Other (unsuccessful) intentions included extensions to Harrow or Tring. Supported by the LNWR, Acts were passed in 1846 for Oxford-Bletchley and Claydon-Buckingham, but with overstretched resources on 22 July 1847 the companies merged into the 'Buckinghamshire Railway' (BuckR). Chaired by Chandos, its provisional committee included eight from the LNWR and up-and-coming secretary Edward Watkin (knighted 1868). An extension was permitted in 1847 from Buckingham to Banbury, but while authorisation for the Claydon-Aylesbury leg was granted in 1851 the LNWR refused to support it (merely duplicating their own branch), and this section was cancelled. Ironically it would later be independently built (p.31).

Under Robert Stephenson as engineer (assisted by R.B. Dockray for the Aylesbury/Banbury sections) and contractors 'Brassey & Company', priority was given to the Buckingham part – likely as the first sod was cut at Buckingham on 20 April 1847, just before the merger. Construction began just after the second 'Mania' so funding suffered from nation-wide hesitation, causing delays. The line's Banbury extension was deferred to 1848 and work stopped outright on the Oxford

Ivatt Class 2 No. 41275 and a BR 'Lightweight' DMU at Buckingham, 1960 – Lamberhurst Collection.*

3edford St Johns Station, 1962 – Lamberhurst Collection.*

line for seven months. In 1849 the Banbury plan was reduced to a single track, the unlaid rails sold to the LNWR. Delays were also caused by local opposition, not helped by the navvies. Their behaviour (as on other lines) stretched local police and the company even funded a Chaplain and moral 'instruction'! The railway did, however, bring much-needed employment luring the national financial crisis. Work sped up by 1850, albeit with two bridges :ollapsing, and the line to Banbury was completed on 25 April. Brassey conducted ı trial run (complete with dinner for 130) before it was ceremonially opened by Verney on 1 May (goods from 15 May). Few boarded the first train, but numbers grew throughout the day and a larger civic event was later held in August.

The Oxford line was completed in stages, opening to Islip (Oxfordshire) on 1 October 1850 and sharing the Bletchley-Claydon Junction track. A temporary erminus opened at Yarnton on 2 December (hoping to meet an ill-fated .BR-proposed Cheltenham line) before the line fully opened to Oxford Rewley Road Station on 20 May 1851 (the GWR blocking access to their station). The irst train was a special excursion to the Hyde Park 'Great Exhibition' with 400 passengers in ten coaches, an official celebration with banquet being held six lays later.

Running four trains daily per line the LNWR leased the routes from 1 July 1851, immediately economising staff numbers. The lines aided local agriculture, particularly the Banbury cattle market and milk to Watford and London, but by 1853 expectations had not been realised. Having anticipated greater through raffic, LNWR fears of GNR competition meant several Bedford-Sandy proposals ailed, in turn hampering the BuckR. Nonetheless, in 1854 the Claydon Junction-Oxford section was doubled (Bletchley-Claydon already double-track) and services increased by 1867 to seven daily Bletchley departures, four splitting at Winslow (then the junction station) for Banbury. In 1868 the ABR reached Claydon

The Bletchley Flyover, 1960 – A. Murray-Rust.*

Claydon Station, 1967 – Lamberhurst Collection.*

Junction, renamed Verney Junction with their new station. Closely affiliatec from the start, the BuckR was finally absorbed into the LNWR on 21 July 1879 the same day as the Bedford Railway.

♦ *Onwards to Cambridge*

Back in Bedfordshire was another unusual but significant little railway. In 185 an estate near Potton was purchased by Captain William Peel (third son of Si Robert Peel PM – and a later VC holder). The 1850 ECML ran through nearby Sandy and Peel saw the benefit of a rail connection for transporting produce Privately purchasing land, so requiring no Act of Parliament, in 1855 constructior began on the 3.5-mile 'Sandy & Potton Railway' (SPR). A grand opening was helc by Lady Peel on 23rd June 1857 with 500-guest banquet and triumphal arch. Pee himself was not present, being ordered to India where he died in 1858 havin never seen his railway. Ownership passed to his brother Arthur Peel. Initially the line was goods-only but after local calls a passenger service began on 8 Novembe 1857 with coaches hired from the GNR. Operation was simple, the four daily

Padbury Station, c.1919 – Lamberhurst Collection.*

Verney Junction, c.1960 – Lamberhurst Collection.*

SPR locomotive Shannon, *named after Captain Peel's frigate – Author with permission from Didcot Railway Centre.*

trains shuttling between termini with trains flagged down wherever needed for potential passengers. Goods remained prevalent (particularly agricultural), some passengers only travelling for the novelty, but it was thought that traffic would improve with a Cambridge extension. Ultimately the SPR only lasted five years, its extension overtaken by another larger proposition.

Numerous Cambridge connections had been proposed but failed, from a Bedford extension in 1846 to an anti-GNR 1847 idea by George Hudson. In 1859 the 'Bedford, Potton & Cambridge Railway' Bill suffered from ECR-GNR hostility (p.93) but, renamed the 'Bedford & Cambridge Railway' (BCR), succeeded in gaining an Act in 1860. For ease the SPR was incorporated in the route, sold in 1861 unusually at a profit. Closed for modification, construction was undertaken by engineer Charles Liddell. There were mixed reactions to the line's viability

'LNWR 'Race to the North' veteran Hardwicke, *a regular Varsity engine post-WWI – Author's Collection.*

(notwithstanding the broader west-east route) especially with the limited local population, reflected in fundraising difficulties. Turning to the LNWR, as the line's operator, £70,000 was granted in return for conditions including three of their Directors on the board, supervision of construction and a guaranteed dividend. Completed three months early, a Directors special ran on 4 July before opening publicly with free rides on 7 July 1862; goods began from 1 August. Initially running four Bedford-Cambridge and one Bedford-Bletchley train daily, traffic was plentiful – additional coaches even once had to be borrowed from the ECR. The three daily goods trains were similarly busy; local agriculture and market gardening flocked to send vegetables to Covent Garden, River Ouse traffic declining. On 5 July 1865 the BCR was absorbed by the LNWR, the final part of the combined west-east route to be taken over.

♦ *The Route*

From Oxford the line ran northeast through Bicester into Buckinghamshire, the gradient on this largely straight section rising to 1 in 142 near Swanbourne. Aside from several bridges and the Wolvercote Tunnel (Oxfordshire) there was little notable civil engineering. Intermediate stations (plus three in Oxfordshire) were at Marsh Gibbon & Poundon (1880), Claydon, Verney Junction (1868), Winslow (opened with the Banbury branch) and Swanbourne before Bletchley: hub of the 77-mile *Varsity Line*. Although there were some west-east through trains, the need to cross all four WCML running lines meant that most services terminated instead, passengers changing to continue their journey.

The Cambridge section continued through Bedford, weaving westwards. Gradients were again difficult, trains occasionally stalling on the steep 1 in 129.5 at Brogborough Hill (even with a cutting – a route deviation avoiding tunnel construction), while the BCR modified the ex-SPR trackbed to help address the

Class 150 'Sprinter' No. 150109 at Bedford Station – M. Buck.*

issue. Alongside associated earthworks were numerous bridges – particularly four before Sandy over the Great Ouse and Ivel Rivers. These later precluded doubling the Bedford-Sandy track unlike Bletchley-Bedford (as-built) and Sandy-Cambridge (completed 1871). Sandy itself was treated as two separate stations on the one site, even having two stationmasters until 1917. Crossing the GNR here via a lattice bridge, this caused a bottleneck preventing quadrupling of the ECML until after the *Varsity Line* closed. Strangely, due to the BCR's S-curve through Sandy, southbound GNR and LNWR trains departed in opposite directions. Bletchley-Bedford intermediate stations in Buckinghamshire were at Fenny Stratford and Woburn (renamed 'Woburn Sands' 1860), then Ridgmont, Lidlington and Millbrook (originally 'Marston', renamed 'Ampthill' 1847, 'Ampthill (Marston)' 1850 and 'Millbrook for Ampthill' 1877-1910) in Bedfordshire. In 1905 new Oxford-Bicester and Bletchley-Bedford halts were added, the latter at Bow Brickhill, Aspley Guise, Husborne Crawley (closed 1941), Wootton Pillinge Halt (minus the 'Halt' from 1928, renamed 'Stewartby' 1935), Wootton Broadmead Halt (closed 1941; officially in 1952), Kempston Hardwick Halt and Kempston Halt ('Kempston & Elstow Halt' from 1908, closed 1941; officially in 1949). After Bedford (renamed 'Bedford St Johns' 1924) were Willington (1903), Blunham, Girtford Halt (1938-40, tickets sold from a nearby garage; closed to goods 1951), Sandy, Potton (re-sited under the BCR) and four in Cambridgeshire.

Lastly, the 21-mile Verney Junction-Banbury branch snaked northwest through the Chiltern hills with light gradients and little civil engineering. Stations (excepting those on the *Varsity Line*) were at Padbury (1878), Buckingham, Radclive Halt (1956) Water Stratford Halt (1956) and Westbury Crossing (1879, renamed 'Fulwell & Westbury' 1880; closed to goods 1951) plus three in Northamptonshire.

As a nationally-significant route, along with the ABR/MET at Verney Junction there were spurs to other lines: the GWR (1940, Oxfordshire), 'Oxford, Worcester & Wolverhampton Railway' (1854, built as the 'Buckinghamshire Junction Railway' but actually in Oxfordshire), GCR (1940) and GNR (1940). Bletchley also gained the south-facing 'Worcester Curve' for Worcester-Euston access (1854-64; reopened 1942). Passing through both agricultural and industrial areas there were also many private sidings, particularly numerous brickworks, and notably to the WWII Bicester Ministry of Defence (MoD) depot with its own military railway. A former livestock siding renamed 'Belle Vue' similarly served a WWII P.O.W. camp at Gamlingay, while Potton was also known for 'coprolite' (prehistoric fossil remains rather than literal dinosaur droppings!) excavated from 1866 for chemical fertiliser.

♦ *Royalty and Runaways*

Many events occurred over these metals from minor to world-changing. It was the crossroads of lines at Bletchley linking Universities that led to the nearby Bletchley Park estate becoming the tenth Secret Intelligence Service code-breaking centre ('Station X'). Supported by the railway, its work was vital to WWII and the development of modern computers. Innumerable university students and staff similarly used the *Varsity Line*, one being Professor C.S. Lewis, author of *The Chronicles of Narnia*. Departing Cambridge he often telephoned Bletchley refreshment room ordering an omelette to be prepared when they saw his train arriving. By the time it pulled in the meal was ready with enough time to eat before his Oxford train... Verney Junction was likewise frequented by Florence Nightingale on regular visits to Claydon House.

The Banbury line was graced several times by the Royal Train, often as part of long-distance travel. On 13 May 1950 King George VI, Queen Elizabeth and Princess Margaret first attended motor racing at Silverstone, disembarking at Brackley. Despite extensive planning the low platform had been overlooked and a box was quickly sourced to aid the unwell monarch in stepping down. On 4 April 1966 a Royal Tour of north Buckinghamshire resulted in the line near Padbury Station becoming overnight home to the Royal Train, Queen Elizabeth II and HRH Prince Philip – despite then being goods-only and the station disused!

Initials of the BCR in the canopy of Potton Station – R. Press.

With its length and heavy usage the lines also saw numerous accidents. In 1909 a goods train was picking up trucks at Padbury when the Guard hitched a lift on the last truck as it cleared the points. However, while stationary the driver had jumped off to pick violets. Not friendly with the fireman, he did not know the latter had already left to answer the call of nature. Whether the regulator was still open or the cylinder cocks leaking is unknown, but the train moved off – Guard finding the crew chasing behind! As he clambered from truck to truck, points at Fulwell were set to divert the runaway from an oncoming passenger service, but before reaching there it came to a halt. Knowing of the passenger train, the Guard swiftly set it in reverse and returned to Buckingham as fast as possible. Ultimately the Guard was rewarded for his actions, while the crew was dismissed.

Swanbourne Station gained a substantial yard during WWII, built on a steep gradient.

Swanbourne Station, 1967 – Lamberhurst Collection.*

The derelict Verney Junction, 2016 – Author.

Trucks occasionally ran away smashing siding buffers; once cleaning up after such an accident a brake van being used to move replacement sleepers was inadvertently bumped. Uncoupled, it also ran away – and with the siding's buffers already destroyed it ended up in the next field! At the other end, a platelayer's hut was behind some buffers with a coach in the siding for equipment. On another occasion the departing Banbury goods train misread the signal and detoured into that siding, crushing the coach and flattening the hut. Luckily, no-one was hurt.

Although not the deadliest, the most serious incident occurred at Bedford on 12 March 1875. The MR and LNWR lines unusually formed a level crossing rather than by bridge or tunnel, but a poorly-placed signal meant stationary LNWR trains fouled the MR main line. Drivers therefore usually did not depart Bedford St John Station until green to avoid this. Unfortunately, this day the driver departed on the guard's whistle, smoke masking the signal but expected to be green as LNWR trains commonly departed before MR ones. It was red. Missing a warning from the signalman, the danger was only realised when the MR train was seen bearing down on them. Trying to outpace it, the engine and three coaches cleared but the fourth was struck squarely and destroyed, the derailed MR engine levelling the signalbox. Three passengers were injured, one fatally. At Trial the driver was found guilty but given leniency (although still dismissed), and the signal repositioned.

More amusingly, pre-WWII Bletchley had a slip coach service off the main line (as did many branches), but occasionally its guard would

Potton Station, 1967 – G. Skelsey.*

accidentally stop short of the platform. Ideally stopping by the exit stairs, one time the Stationmaster angrily admonished a guard, declaring '*Tomorrow I will stand near the stairs with a red light and stop right opposite*'. The following day he was there with the light, but the slip coach stopped before even reaching the station. The sly guard quoted regulations to the furious Stationmaster: a red hand lamp was a danger signal so he had halted the coach immediately!

♦ *The Varsity Line*

Now all under LNWR operation, the sections were unified to form the university-linking *Varsity Line* and the secondary Banbury branch. They were well used: five Bletchley-Oxford, five Bletchley-Cambridge, two Bletchley-Bedford and six Bletchley-Banbury trains daily by 1882, later including three daily Oxford-Cambridge through expresses from 1905. Excursions were common, later holidays to the coast, plus Cambridge race meet traffic – both people and horses. Goods similarly flourished, not just local supplies (agriculture, bricks and coal)

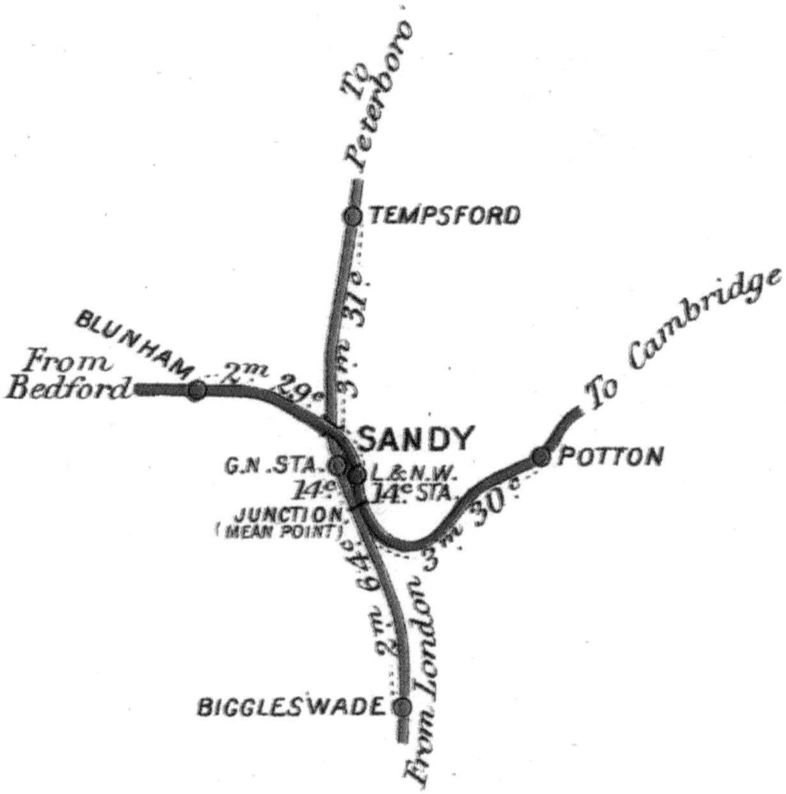

The railways of Sandy, 1914 – Railway Clearing House.*

but through trains such as from the Eastern Counties. Improving local services further, in 1905 railmotors were introduced with new halts. These temporarily ceased c.1917-19, and while the Oxford railmotor ended outright in 1926 with the General Strike the Bedford service continued with push-pull trains dubbed the 'Bedford Motor'. The Banbury line never had the same extent of traffic as the *Varsity Line*, even with Banbury-bound GWR iron ore and special excursions, peaking around WWI – aided by the Banbury munitions factory.

Falling under the LMS in 1923, by the 1930s there were two Oxford-Cambridge, ten Oxford-Bletchley, 17 Bletchley-Cambridge (including Bletchley-Bedford shuttle) and five Bletchley-Banbury services daily. Experimental railcars visited on test, notably a 1932 Michelin petrol railcar – a 10-wheel bus-like unit using pneumatic tyres for the first time in Britain – and a short-lived Stanier streamlined three-car unit in 1938. WWII massively boosted traffic, the *Varsity Line* becoming a vital if increasingly congested route. Spurs to other main lines enabled use as a detour route; there were regular troop and ambulance trains, supplies (especially with Bicester depot) and a secretive Bedford service for Bletchley Park workers known as 'The Whitehall'. Additional facilities were also built, including several petrol dumps, although three halts closed in 1941.

Traffic diminished with Peace, post-war road usage an ever-increasing threat. The Bletchley-Banbury line saw reduced services, only three daily trains by 1952, and decreasing farming traffic compounded by lost milk trade after a 1955 strike. Losing £14,000 annually, efforts were still made to encourage passengers. In 1956 as a test of BR's 'Modernisation Plan', Banbury-Buckingham railcars were introduced (the remainder steam) with two additional halts. This proved massively successful – passenger traffic increased 400% and on some market days the two units had to be coupled together to create enough space. Even so it was not considered sufficient, and on 2 January 1961 the Buckingham-Banbury portion closed to passengers. The railcars were transferred to the surviving Bletchley-Buckingham section but inclusion in the Beeching Report spelled the end, this service ending on 7 September 1964. Goods continued to Banbury and Buckingham, but the line finally closed on 5 December 1966, track-lifting commencing in 1967.

The *Varsity Line* had similar challenges, Oxford Rewley Road closing on 1 October 1951 (trains terminating at the GWR station), but its west-east route offered a saving grace. In 1956 an upgrade was proposed for studying cross-country connections outside of London. Central to it was a flyover at Bletchley enabling non-stop through operation without fouling the main line. Opened on 15 January 1962 at a cost of £1.5 million the project evaporated, and by 1981 it was traversed by only four trains a week. It was never used by any passenger service. Closure was first mooted in 1959, protests instead leading to cost-saving dieselisation, and local support deferred service modifications (closing intermediate stations) threatened in the Beeching Report. A third closure attempt in July 1964 was suspended for public enquiry, but losing £100,000 annually this reprieve would not last. Running ten trains daily by 1967, on 30 December the final train departed, nearly empty and marked only by a few detonators.

Sandy Station, 1966 – G. Skelsey.*

Passenger services officially ceased on 1 January 1968. Goods continued on the Oxford line, Oxford-Bicester singled in 1973 with the rest in 1985, but passengers briefly returned (railtours notwithstanding) with Christmas shopping specials to Winslow in 1984. The Bedford-Cambridge section, conversely, closed outright (lifted in 1969) with only a short spur remaining from Bedford to Goldington power station until 1981.

The Bletchley-Bedford part, however, would be very different. Dieselised with the rest of the line in 1959 (halt platforms having to be raised), insufficient alternate bus transport forced BR to maintain the shuttle service. Closure was reconsidered in 1972 but protests and bus problems protected the line, local support creating the 'Bedford to Bletchley Rail Users' Association' in 1980. Brick traffic peaked in the 1960s, the 'London Brick Company' site at Stewartby the largest in the world, but despite gaining a miniature railfreight depot in 1974 rail usage ceased in 1985. Bedford St Johns Station was re-sited in the former yard on 14 May 1984, trains terminating at the ex-MR Bedford Station, and since Privatisation services reached 16 trains daily by 2010.

♦ *The Lines Today*

Much of the trackbed now forms field borders, and few buildings remain. A Banbury line cutting, used as a 1970s landfill, forms part of the Farthinghoe Nature Reserve while the trackbed through Buckingham is now the *Railway Walk*. Bedford-Sandy is likewise a cyclepath. Unusually, a section within Cambridgeshire is now part of the 'Mullard Radio Astronomy Observatory', a telescope traversing the line via a 20-foot gauge track. Of the Oxford section much remains mothballed, the ex-GCR link used for 'Binliner' rubbish trains to Calvert until 2021. Oxford-Bicester was reopened to passengers by 'Network SouthEast' in 1987, Gavray Junction later connecting to the ex-GWGCJR *Chiltern Line* enabling London-Oxford services. Bletchley-Bedford, now the *Marston Vale Line*, operates under 'London Northwestern' with hourly services. Supported by the Marston Vale Community Rail Partnership', they also run the 'Ridgmont Station Heritage Centre'. Future plans for the *Varsity Line* have been heavily discussed, notably the 'East-West Rail' project. Having already reopened the Oxford end and started preparations for a new Winslow Station (2023) its intention is linking it back to Bletchely and Bedford before ultimately reconnecting with Cambridge and beyond – a bright future for this once-important route.

The Wycombe Railway

Despite the *Varsity Line* the rest of Buckinghamshire was at first poorly served by the railways. The Wycombe Railway (WR), however, changed this, growing into a substantial micro-network radiating from High Wycombe to Maidenhead, Princes Risborough, Aylesbury and Oxford. While linking other lines, its primary function was provincial: opening a new region, serving the county and aiding in its wider development. Such was its value that surviving parts remain integral to the Chiltern network.

♦ *Growing Ambitions*

The WR was formed in 1845, proposing a line from High Wycombe to the GWR at Maidenhead. Championed by the GWR an Act was passed in 1846, becoming a named exception to the subsequent Railway Regulation (Gauge) Act 1846 preventing broad gauge expansion outside of southwest England and Wales.

Aylesbury Station, 1991 – B. Brooksbank.*

Unlikely workmates: BR Classes 121 and 68 at Princes Risborough – S. Mulligan.

GWR support even led to the line's first engineer being none other than I.K Brunel. Construction was nonetheless delayed through financial issues, in 184 even trying to sell land to the GWR – blocked by an Act preventing 'premature sale of incomplete railways. Work finally started in 1852, the lapsed Act havin to be revived, but the hoped-for 1853 opening was further impeded not just b finances but the contractors going bankrupt. The line finally opened on 1 Augus 1854, being immediately leased to the GWR. Through services commenced fron Paddington with further trains starting at Maidenhead.

Plainly successful and on the edge of untapped territory, the ambitious W looked to expansion. An 1857 Act granted an extension to Princes Risboroug but this was only part of a larger plan. 1861 saw authorisation for two furthe extensions from Princes Risborough (becoming a notable junction) to Oxford an Aylesbury. The former opened as far as Thame (Oxfordshire) on 1 August 1862 marked by a Directors special. Work began almost immediately on the next stage reaching Kennington Junction on the GWR Oxford line on 24 October 1864 Initial services comprised four daily trains from Princes Risborough, growin to six by 1886. The Aylesbury extension opened on 1 October 1863, again wit no ceremony. Its terminus was Aylesbury's second station (the line not meetin the LNWR branch; p.88), which was shared from 1868 with the ABR (later MET p.31). Originally there were four daily trains from Princes Risborough.

On 1 February 1867 the WR was amalgamated into the GWR, and while th extensions were profitable a problem arose. The position of broad gauge wa faltering, and the difficulty of potential mixed gauge track at Aylesbury with th ABR triggered conversion of the Aylesbury-Princes Risborough line to standar

;auge. One of the shortest-ived broad gauge lines (only ive years), this became the ;WR's first broad-to-standard egauging. Conducted over 14-23)ctober 1868 the work over-ran y two days, a temporary mnibus operating during the rocess (an early rail replacement us!). Unfortunately the finished ine was now severed from the est of the broad gauge GWR, nd the remainder of the ex-WR vas regauged from 23 August to : September 1870.

The complexity of dual-gauge track – Author, with permission from Didcot Railway Centre.

The local value of these lines was substantial. Southern Buckinghamshire ;ained superior access to London, Oxford, Birmingham and western England ılongside multiple main lines to areas as far as southern Wales. Rail development :ontinued further, with links to the 1872 Watlington and 1873 Marlow branches p.125). Paper mills grew up around Wycombe – a key part of the limited goods raffic, some having private sidings. The famous Wycombe chair-making industry :onversely refused to use the railway, fearing damage or theft, remaining with oad transport until the twentieth century. Passenger traffic became pivotal, by 1872 having 11 daily London trains: nine to Paddington and two to Victoria.

.oudwater Station, c.1915 – Lamberhurst Collection.*

♦ *The Routes*

GWR Prairie No. 6118 from High Wycombe meets No. 6593 Leighton Hall *at Maidenhead, 1953 – B. Brooksbank*.*

Starting at Maidenhead, the 18-mile single track curved northeast towards Bourne End, crossing Cock Marsh and the River Thames via the line's largest structure. Akin to his Cornish work, Brunel designed a wooden viaduct crossing the marsh (later replaced with an embankment) and a further 12-arch wooden bridge for the river. A source of construction delays and awkward for river traffic, this was replaced in 1895 by a three-span steel bridge. Following th Wye River Valley there was a rising gradient as it neared the parallel GWGCJI line, these lines merging at High Wycombe. At first WR trains used their owr independent 'Maidenhead (Wycombe Branch)' Station (renamed 'Maidenheac Boyne Hill' 1866), closed on 1 November 1871 with the opening of the mair line's Maidenhead Station. Subsequent WR stations were Furze Platt (1937; a hal until 1969), Cookham, Bourne End ('Marlow Road' until 1874), Wooburn Greer ('Woburn Green' until 1872), Loudwater and High Wycombe ('Wycombe' until 1864). As the line expanded, further stations opened at West Wycombe (closed to passengers 1958, outright 1963), Saunderton (1901) and Princes Risborough.

No. 6022 King Edward III *speeds through Princes Risborough, 1961 – B. Brooksbank*.*

Continuing 7 miles towards Aylesbury, stations were at Monks Risborough & Whiteleaf Halt (1929, renamed 'Monks Risborough' from 1974), Little Kimble (1872) and South Aylesbury Halt (1933-67). The gradient fell 1 in 50 just prior to this halt; when used for MGCJR diversions heavy trains found it a distinct challenge.

The 30-mile single-track Thame line travelled west from Princes Risborough briefly parallel to the Watlington branch, little actually being within Buckinghamshire. The only notable civil engineering was in Oxfordshire, warranting the Horspath Tunnel and Kennington Bridge. Stations were at Bledloe, Towersey Halt (1937) and eight further in Oxfordshire (including four 1908 halts).

♦ *A Varied Fate*

Once established, railway operations were largely uneventful, concentrating on local services until the twentieth century. The GCR's London extension opened in 1899, through goods trains taking advantage of the Aylesbury-Maidenhead route (bypassing much of the MET – to their annoyance, even going to court) until 1900 and the GWR-GCR Banbury link. More significantly in 1906 the GWGCJR opened, the Princes Risborough-High Wycombe stretch absorbed into this newly-constructed main line (being duly upgraded and doubled in 1892). The line north to Aylesbury, though remaining a branch, was placed under this committee, Aylesbury Station itself coming under both GWGCJR and MGCJR from 1907. With a more direct main line to Paddington and Marylebone, the WR's original London purpose was supplanted and traffic fell. Ironically it simultaneously grew in operational value as an alternate link between the GWR and GCR, while local demand ensured continuing operation (particularly with its branch connections). The 1910 GWR Aynho Line (p.39) further redirected WR traffic, services now capable of bypassing Oxford, and intended Thame line upgrades were cancelled.

By the 1930s the rise of fashionable suburbs and commuting around Maidenhead and Aylesbury, coupled with decreasing passenger traffic on the Thame line (even with an additional thrice-daily Princes Risborough-Thame railmotor by 1922), had led to new halts and stations as encouragement. In 1937 there were 12 daily trains on the Maidenhead section, 15 Aylesbury trains and seven on the Thame line. The Aylesbury stretch had no stopping goods, stations having no goods facilities, but the Thame line benefitted from wartime goods and from the 1920s the Oxfordshire Morris Cowley motor factory. During WWII it saw ambulance trains to a US military hospital near Wheatley (Oxfordshire) and occasional Worcester expresses when other lines were damaged. In 1941 the line gained female staff (albeit temporarily), one employed as a guard recalling a heavily-sparking engine pulling what turned out to be a munitions train!

Problems, however, began in the 1960s. Growing road competition accelerated decline across the ex-WR, services diminishing. The Watlington branch closed in 1957 and closure of the Thame line was 'under investigation' by 1959. From 1961 DMUs began operation, steam finally disappearing when Oxford shed closed in 1966. Beeching's Report further revealed that alongside the Thame line, the Princes Risborough-Banbury passenger service had also been previously investigated for withdrawal. More importantly the Report killed the ex-GCR main line, so reducing traffic over the Princes Risborough-High Wycombe section.

Considering the WR's fate, the Maidenhead-High Wycombe section continued services (including some London through trains) but decreased in importance, goods ceasing c.1966-7. Loudwater and Wooburn Green were relegated to halts in 1968, and despite a new short-lived 1967-70 Maidenhead-High Wycombe train, services diminished until 5 May 1969 when the Maidenhead-Aylesbury train was withdrawn. Requiring £60,000 to keep running, the Ministry of Transport refused BR the funds, so on 2 May 1970 the last train passed. Two days later, with little public reaction, the central Bourne End-High Wycombe part closed. It was used to train permanent way staff for two years before being lifted.

Bledlow Station, 1961 – B. Brooksbank.*

Ex-GCR services ended in 1966 but Princes Risborough-High Wycombe continued operation as part of the down-graded Marylebone-Banbury line while the Aylesbury line retained five trains by 1971. Both of these changed from Western to London Midland Region in 1974 before becoming part of 'Network SouthEast's 1985 *Chiltern Line* (p.43).

The Thame line might have offered the shortest London-Oxford route, but by 1962 was losing £26,000 annually. On 7 January 1963 passenger services ceased (before Beeching's Report was published), the last train having a passenger in mourning clothes. Through goods trains continued until 1967 when repairs to Horspath Tunnel were deemed uneconomic. Closed between Thame and Horspath Halt in 1968, the extremities retained traffic, however, with a Thame oil terminal being served until 12 April 1991. Thereafter the Princes Risborough-Thame section closed, being lifted in 1998.

♦ *Division and Dignitaries*

Such was the power of company competition that construction of the Thame extension led to an unusual situation. The GWR had an unofficial agreement with the Oxfordshire-Monmouthshire 'West Midland Railway' not to support or build lines nearby without consultation. Although the WR did not strictly apply, the impoverished company saw the opportunity for profit by stoking GWR-LNWR rivalries.

Promoting a new competing line from Yarnton to London with an Aylesbury branch, it backfired spectacularly: the LNWR had no interest and barely two years later in 1863 the company was taken over by the GWR. Other companies also encountered difficulties, turnpike roads in particular. The Beaconsfield to Stokenchurch turnpike ceased in 1867, its route largely duplicated (and lengthened) by the WR. The Buckingham to Hanwell turnpike similarly ceased in 1871.

The line had various notable visitors, such as in 1864 when Queen Victoria's son the Prince of Wales (later Edward VII) visited the Earl of Macclesfield. Saunderton Station conversely was burned down by Suffragettes in 1913. More recently in 1998 Little Kimble Station hosted the Royal Train during the G8 Summit, being close to Chequers. Unexpected 'VIPs' caused confusion there in 2010, however, when the ticket machine became home to a family of protected *Glis glis* edibile dormice…!

◆ *Trains and Trails*

Today much of the former WR remains operational. After being severed the Maidenhead-Bourne End portion stayed viable thanks to the Marlow connection, essentially becoming part of that branch. Princes Risborough-High Wycombe is now operated by 'Chiltern Railways' within their London-Birmingham *Chiltern Line*, as is the Princes Risborough-Aylesbury section. Alongside an hourly Marylebone service this has a peak-time Aylesbury-Princes Risborough shuttle. Thame line goods trains continue in Oxfordshire between Kennington Junction and the Morris Cowley factory.

As for where closed, the Thame-Princes Risborough trackbed now forms the *Phoenix Way* cyclepath. Parts of the High Wycombe-Bourne End trackbed similarly became a conservation footpath – protection after encroaching c.1970-80s redevelopment. Reopening has been frequently discussed, feasibility studies undertaken, but despite government lobbying under the 2020 'Restoring Your Railway' fund the former WR looks set to remain divided.

Bridging Four Main Lines

Forming a west-east route across southern Bedfordshire and Hertfordshire were four branches spanning the LNWR, MR, GNR and GER main lines. Just as notable as the *Varsity* and Wycombe lines they, however, remained administratively and operationally separate. This lack of through running significantly limited their potential, remaining provincial branches destined to their varied fates.

The NER Hertford Branch

The first railway to serve Hertfordshire's county town, also connecting three other lines, it became the easternmost part of this larger cross-county route. Although originating in competition rather than fulfilling any particular need, it would nonetheless prove its worth – remaining of value even amid 1960s closures.

◆ *Origins and Opposition*

The NER main line towards Cambridge reached Broxbourne in 1840, its construction slow with competitors seeking to take advantage through rival schemes – in particular a counter-proposal for a Cambridge line via Ware. The rurality north of London dissuaded building branches, but with their line threatened there would be legal rights if the company had a stake in this area. A connection to the county town would also tap into the significant local barley and malt trade. In 1841 the 'Hertford & Ware Railway' received assent, blocking the rival plan in what would be one of the NER's last projects. As advisory Chief Engineer Robert Stephenson oversaw construction, undertaken by contractors 'Grissel & Peto'. Company finances were always poor though and construction was delayed, locals fearing it would not reach Hertford. This was compounded by the 'Cheshunt Turnpike Trust' and its surveyor, James McAdam (son of iconic roadbuilder John McAdam).

A Class 305 at Hertford East, 1979 – Dr N. Clifton.*

A viaduct was built at Ware to detour the Great Cambridge Road over the railway, but this was still incomplete when in October 1843 the NER considered opening the line. McAdam insisted the viaduct be finished before tracks crossed the turnpike at Amwell End, then the only north-south access road. However, work began immediately after this meeting and a level crossing was completed overnight, to the surprise of residents the next day! The turnpike trust took the NER to Court, demanding the track's removal within seven days. Peto responded stating the viaduct could be complete in a fortnight but wanted a certificate of approval from McAdam – no certificate and the crossing would be immediately re-laid and trains begun. Backing down, a BoT inspection was held on 26 October 1843 and with little ceremony the line opened on 31 October. Turnpike issues remained – the viaduct was still unfinished due to connection issues with nearby roads. It was only with the 1845 replacement of the Ware Bridge over the River Lea (amid further criticisms continuing to 1848) that the matter was finally resolved. Originally there were seven trains running daily through to London and traffic developed well, Hertford despite its small size being an economic focal point.

Leased to the ECR in 1844, the 5-foot gauge track was re-laid to standard gauge over 25 April to 30 September 1844, a horse omnibus standing in while closed. In 1846 the track was doubled, all bar a section through Ware as the 'New River Company' refused to sell more land (plus the ongoing turnpike issues). Although numerous extension plans failed the Buntingford branch opened in 1863 (later sharing London-bound tracks; p.105), while in 1858 Hertford gained a second railway from Welwyn complete with ECR connection (p.75). Joint-run by the GNR and ECR until 1860 this link could have formed a Welwyn-Broxbourne bypass around London, but the Hatfield junction layout precluded any such use, instead only ever being used for goods.

Although traffic was expanding, particularly malting, the ECR was in increasingly dire straits. Ridiculed and in debt, it even charged one Mr Cox for traveling without a ticket – despite being Rye House Stationmaster! In 1862 it amalgamated into the GER (although the leasing NER remained independent

The platelayer's friend: a Wickham inspection trolley – S. Mulligan.

until 1902), the branch's third operator in only nineteen years. Hertford's markets and industry continued to grow, and on 27 February 1888 Hertford GER Station was moved closer to the town centre. The former station became a goods depot until the 1960s. Services rose from 11 daily trains in 1874 to 24 by 1892 (including 12 to Liverpool Street and one to St Pancras, arranged with the MR), but traffic levels would be challenged in 1924 with the opening of the GNR's 'Hertford Loop' (p.24).

◆ *The Route*

Nearly 7 miles long (excluding GNR connection), it passed northwest from Broxbourne, curving to follow the Lea Valley. The junction was a mile north of this station, the branch largely running between the Lea Navigation and 1613 'New River' with little substantial civil engineering. Stations after Broxbourne were at Rye House (unofficially from 1845, officially 1846), St Margaret's, Ware and Hertford ('Hertford East' from 1923, the branch similarly renamed).

◆ *Wickhams of Ware*

The line had many private sidings, including Rye House power station, concrete plants, a gravel works (with internal tramway) and Chadwell Biscuit Factory. Most famous, however, was the Ware-based manufacturer 'D. Wickham &

Company'. Beginning in 1886 as a car and general engineering firm, from 1922 they constructed railway equipment, becoming best known for rail inspection vehicles. Built to various gauges in their hundreds, these were used by the 'Big Four' alongside owners worldwide. Railcars were also constructed, mostly for export but with some briefly used in Britain such as the Class 109. With a new factory in 1935 and tank repairs during WWII – transported by rail – the company made an agreement with the LNER to test some of their export items locally, notably on the Buntingford branch but also at least once to Hertford and Stevenage. The firm ceased trading in 1991, but many items can still be found in regular operation.

◆ *Collision!*

Rye House was a stop before any station, tickets being sold at a nearby hotel to fishing club members. An official station opened on 31 May 1846 but a platform was only constructed in 1849 to test the viability of the location. Henry Teale of Rye House supported the station (some claiming he also fiddled the passenger receipts) and the House grew to be a major tourist attraction until the 1930s. Hertford's first station conversely was located to keep it distant from Christ's Hospital School and the County Gaol. Unfortunately it suffered several robberies in 1844, culminating in nearly all the staff being fired!

Various incidents have occurred on the branch, some with unfortunate consequences. In January 1847 a man grew impatient waiting at Ware level crossing and tried to pass. The crossing keeper was punched in the face attempting to stop him, and moments later the man was struck by a train, losing both legs. More happily, on 15 May 1912 gate-porter David Wheal saw an elderly

Ware Station, 2009 – B. Brooksbank.*

lady crossing the track unaware of an oncoming train. Rushing out he pushed her clear, being rewarded by the GER, the Carnegie Hero Fund and receiving the Edward Medal for bravery.

The most significant incident though was at Ware. The only single-track stretch, there was an unofficial practice at St Margaret's of using a flag or lamp to inform the driver if they were continuing under 'Regulation 3' (section clear) or 'Regulation 5' (section clear but station blocked). On 31 October 1927 the late-running 7:18pm Hertford train departed St Margaret's amid thickening mist. Its driver assumed he was following 'Regulation 3' but was actually under 'Regulation 5' (despite being forbidden during fog). Meanwhile the 8:43pm London-bound train entered Ware Station, shortly departing again. As the Hertford train neared Ware it overshot the 'down' home signal and entered the single track. Realising the error and applying the brakes, its crew sighted the oncoming London train. At 8:49pm they collided head-on at a combined speed of 15mph. Although staying on the rails the engines were badly damaged while the coaches telescoped and many smashed apart. Although gas-lit no fire occurred and amazingly of the 51 people involved only 27 were injured and none were killed. The ensuing investigation was very critical, particularly of the Ware signalman and Hertford train driver, highlighting the laxities that had built up with staff that had spent their entire careers on the line. Ironically another collision would occur during WWII – partially the result of the wartime blackout.

♦ *Post-Grouping to Present*

Coming under the LNER post-Grouping, by 1927 there were 26 daily passenger services and a further four goods trains. Rising post-War road competition led to the closures of the GNR and Buntingford branches, but Hertford remained a notable commuter and industrial area. Even with potential competition from the 'Hertford Loop' the branch not only retained economic value but also the prospect of future growth. The Rye House-Hertford stretch was electrified on 25 April 1960, Class 305 Electric Multiple Units (EMUs) being tested, with the remainder completed as part of the suburban *Lea Valley Lines* network on 21 November 1960. Services beyond Broxbourne thereafter used the re-commissioned 'Southbury Loop' (p.137), goods continuing to Hertford North via the former GNR connection until closed in 1966. Branch goods traffic still remained, only ceasing with the closure of the last sidings in 1991. Coming under the 'West Anglia' section of 'Network SouthEast' until Privatisation, today the branch is operated by 'Greater Anglia' with a half-hourly London service (20 minutes at peak). With plans for increased capacity, its future promises continuation as a key Hertfordshire commuter route.

The LNWR Leighton-Dunstable Branch

The next part constructed of this cross-county route was at the other end, connecting the WCML to Dunstable in Bedfordshire. While particularly important for local goods, the 'Dunstable Dasher' became a casualty of modernisation with its full potential never fully realised.

LNWR Coal Tank No. 1054, formerly based at Bletchley – S. Mulligan.

♦ *Argumentative Beginnings*

During the nineteenth century Luton rose as Bedfordshire's leading industrial centre, particularly noted for straw hatting. By the 1850s it was Britain's largest town without rail or waterway connection. Leighton on the LBR was its nearest station and in 1841 a scheme was proposed for a branch to Luton via Dunstable. Planned by no less than George and Robert Stephenson it was initially greatly supported, but this was short-lived. Intending to cross the 'Great Moor', common land by the River Lea, this and its lesser branch status was increasingly criticised. On 11 May 1844 George Stephenson attended a public meeting at Luton's *George Hotel* which concluded with the plan's absolute rejection. Furious, Stephenson vowed he would never return and Luton would not gain a railway while he lived. Coincidentally, both would become true.

The LBR persisted, proposing a loop via Dunstable, in turn being cut back to a simple branch. The 'Dunstable & London & Birmingham Railway' gained assent in 1845, granting sufficient in shares to cover land acquisition and construction (even some operation). There was another Luton extension plan to Watford in 1845, but this again failed to materialise. In the meantime the LNWR was formed, purchasing the branch on completion. The line opened to goods on 29 May 1848 and passengers on 1 June. Well frequented, it helped trigger another – successful – Luton railway. With a junction authorised to the LNWR branch, the GNR-supported 'Luton, Dunstable & Welwyn Junction Railway' (LDWJR;

p.76) opened in 1858 – ironically creating in essence Stephenson's original plan. BoT inspection insisted on a turntable at Leighton, and at first only the Luton-Dunstable part was operational. The LNWR therefore ran trains on its behalf via their branch, mostly Dunstable-Luton services but with two daily Leighton-Luton trains. Particularly encouraging commuting between Leighton and Dunstable, this boosted their own passenger numbers.

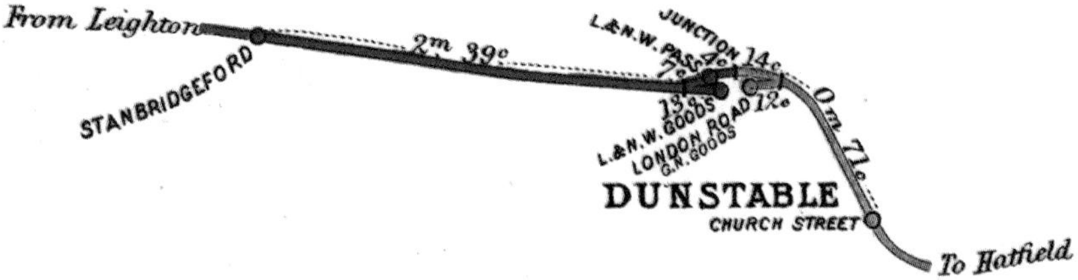

The railways of Dunstable, 1914 – Railway Clearing House.*

Unfortunately, Dunstable Station would cause its own problems. LDWJR services were to terminate at the LNWR Dunstable Station, but this was built at ground level by Watling Street and Parliament forbade connection via a level crossing. The Luton line consequently crossed the road by bridge, bypassing it to a junction further to the west. Trains from Luton therefore had to overshoot and reverse into Dunstable Station or omit it entirely. Plainly inconvenient, the LNWR asked the GNR (as operators) to fund a replacement station, who responded with an offer of rebuilding their own Dunstable Church Street Station instead. The LNWR accepted if they could have equal running rights within the station, which was soundly refused. Bickering continued past completion of the Luton-Welwyn section in September 1860 (LDWJR services reverting to the GNR), and their 1861 takeover of that line. The matter was only finally resolved in January 1866 when the LNWR demoted their terminus to a goods depot and built a new through station on the higher connecting track.

Most passenger services comprised a push-pull Leighton-Dunstable shuttle connecting with GNR trains; five daily when opened rising to seven by 1906. Unlike most other lines (often at a reduced rate), there were no Sunday services – restricted by a landowner. Trains to Luton only restarted in April 1881, continuing till closure. May 1883 to November 1884 also saw a short-lived Luton-Bletchley service. Passenger traffic was steady but unexceptional, its peak being excursions including to Luton Football Club matches. Although the combined route connected the WCML and ECML there were no through services – a missed opportunity.

Goods traffic conversely was of particular local importance. Much comprised market garden produce from around Stanbridgeford, plus substantial quantities of coal to Dunstable gasworks. More important than passengers, at Leighton the junction faced northwards for Midlands goods rather than allowing direct London trains. Private sidings served local industries such as Waterlow's Printing

The Leighton Buzzard narrow-gauge railway – S. Mulligan.

Works and several lime works, while exchange sidings met the Totternhoe Quarries' internal railway. Arguably most significant though was the sand industry, a major undertaking with many local pits around Leighton. Such was its quality that it was used for the glass of the 1851 'Crystal Palace'. Continually expanding, Grovebury Sidings became a key transhipment centre but the roads were increasingly damaged, especially with rising WWI demand. Peace led to cheap ex-War Department equipment and in 1919 the narrow gauge 'Leighton Buzzard Light Railway' opened bringing sand to Grovebury Sidings. With seven branch sand trains daily at its 1930s height WWII reaffirmed the need for both railways, remaining a major goods source until 1967.

♦ *The Route*

The 7-mile line was double-track, running west from Leighton via Stanbridgeford (1849 but only timetabled from 1860) to Dunstable (renamed 'Dunstable North' 1950). Crossing the River Ouzel and GJC much was level with little civil engineering, although with gradients at each end. Leighton fell 1 in 80, but the greater challenge was the 1 in 40 rise to Dunstable. The LBR had first intended an extreme 1 in 27 rope incline, but under the LNWR this was rationalised for locomotives. Even so it was still difficult for heavy goods trains.

♦ *Tracks and Tourism*

Gradients were a major issue, especially for goods trains, and some needed banking into Dunstable. While some trains occasionally stuck, one driver avoided this embarrassment by moving slowly while the fireman walked alongside the engine sanding the track using a watering can! With similar perseverance, in 1945 elderly 1886-built branch Coal Tank No. 7742 was requisitioned to rescue a failed main-line express, returning to Leighton working flat-out at 10mph towing a Jubilee Class and ten coaches...

Watford Tank No. 6917 at Leighton Buzzard, bound for Dunstable, 1948 – B. Brooksbank.*

Passengers had a narrow escape on Boxing Day 1873 in the branch's most serious incident. The 11:05am train from Dunstable had passed Grovebury Crossing when it suddenly derailed. Still moving it stayed upright until it neared the canal, when a carriage broke free and rolled down the embankment, smashing apart. Another coach followed, landing upright. Although 20 passengers were trapped, nine injured, amazingly there were no fatalities. It transpired that platelayers undertaking repairs earlier had moved ballast supporting the sleepers, accidentally weakening the track.

More pleasantly, Stanbridgeford grew as a location for local tourism. Once in 1919 some 700 people arrived back at Stanbridgeford Station, the Stationmaster having to call for extra coaches to get them to Leighton. After closure Stanbridgeford had a final moment in the limelight, in 1968 featuring in *Noon Doomsday*, an episode of *The Avengers*.

LNWR G2 No. 49403 at Leighton Buzzard, c.1960 – Lamberhurst Collection.*

♦ *After the Grouping*

Coming under the LMS, WWII increased traffic – from tanks to troop and ambulance trains. Goods continued, unusually including exotic animals after the opening of Whipsnade Zoo in 1931. Passenger numbers, however, had already diminished and worsened with post-war roads. By the 1950s and BR there were just four trains daily and, reducing to three, the decision was made to withdraw passenger services. Carrying around 300 passengers, the final train – steam hauled with a headboard proclaiming the 'Last Dasher' – departed on 30 June 1962. Two days later passenger trains officially ceased. This was not the end for Dunstable North Station though, continuing to operate under the Hatfield branch. Two further trains would also run: enthusiast railtours in 1962 and 1964. Now goods-only, Stanbridgeford closed outright in 1964 but quarry traffic continued until a pipeline was installed in 1965. Goods traffic between Grovebury Sidings and Dunstable temporarily ended on 1 January 1966, made permanent on 12 June 1967. Severed at Grovebury, the branch closed and tracklifting slowly began in 1968.

Leighton-Grovebury goods continued, but a 1955 rail strike had forced the sand quarries onto the roads and this traffic ended on 8 February 1967. By then under one-engine operation, level crossings had to be opened by the crew themselves. The construction of the new Euston Station gave a brief respite, tipping excavated soil, and there were thoughts of electrification but with the line losing £26,000 annually it was doomed to close. The last train was on 5 December 1969, Class 47 diesel No. 47564 *Colossus* collecting a container wagon (the container purchased by the preserved narrow gauge railway), and on 8 December the branch finally closed. Piecemeal tracklifting continued until the last was removed in 1971.

Two ex-Leighton branch signalboxes survive on the Whipsnade Zoo narrow-gauge railway – Author, with permission from ZSL Whipsnade.

♦ *Vanished Traces*

Near Leighton Buzzard the trackbed is now a cycleway, while a section was used for the A505 Leighton-Linslade Southern Bypass. The remainder from Stanbridgeworth is part of the *Sewell Greenway*, a cyclepath incorporating a nature reserve around the Sewell Cutting. While Leighton Buzzard remains operational, rebuilt over the old trackbed, Dunstable North conversely is long gone – now the offices of Central Bedfordshire Council. By its car park, a semi-circular wall marks the site of the former turntable. Although partly demolished, elements of Stanbridgeworth Station survive as a private residence – one of the few reminders left of this lost branch.

The Hertford, Luton & Dunstable Railway

Completing this west-east route, Dunstable and Hertford were joined by two initially-independent lines. Remaining sleepy branches overshadowed by competing routes, and despite intentions destined never to be physically connected, they still realised a valuable role in this cross-county corridor.

Hertford Cowbridge Station, c.1908 – Lamberhurst Collection.*

♦ *Early Optimism*

The ECML opened in 1850 and there was immediate interest at securing the new territory around Hatfield, pre-empting competing MR expansion. A branch to Hertford gained assent in 1847 (another to Dunstable cut back to St Albans), but with the collapse of the second 'Mania' these proposals vanished. Another GNR-linked line was subsequently mooted by local and London businessmen in 1853, the 'Hertford & Welwyn Junction Railway', granted an Act in 1854. The GNR had already expressed interest in running the line, but with connections to Digswell (Welwyn) and the ECR's Hertford branch running powers were granted to both companies.

Opening to goods on 28 February 1858 and passengers on 1 March, goods proved successful – linked to the ECR branch the GNR was granted powers to Ware so gaining access to London's docks. A promised dock on the local Lea Navigation (to protect river trade) was, however, suspiciously absent. Passenger traffic was more limited as while there were some through bookings the ECR branch was quicker to London. An 1852 truce between the companies prevented excessive competition for the limited Hertford trade and so, keen to maintain this, the branch was run by joint committee. Running five trains daily, extended ECR services beyond Hertford GNR Station (known as Cowbridge) were considered but not undertaken.

Meanwhile, another line was developing. The 'Luton, Dunstable & Welwyn Junction Railway' (LDWJR) was a separate company but shared many promoters. As a consequence they collaborated with the hope of joining tracks, its Act of 1855 including a connecting bridge over the GNR main line. Again the GNR offered to run the branch, but would not provide financial assistance. Connecting Digswell and Dunstable, linking the LNWR, GNR and ECR, authorisation was given for these three to work the line on completion. Following the 1844 Stephenson debacle and a failed 1853 proposal to the GNR, Luton had relied on roads, coaches to London taking nine hours, so the new railway was cause for celebration. The first sod was cut on 25 October 1855 amid heavy rain and the day declared a general holiday, although the local newspaper publicised the wrong day!

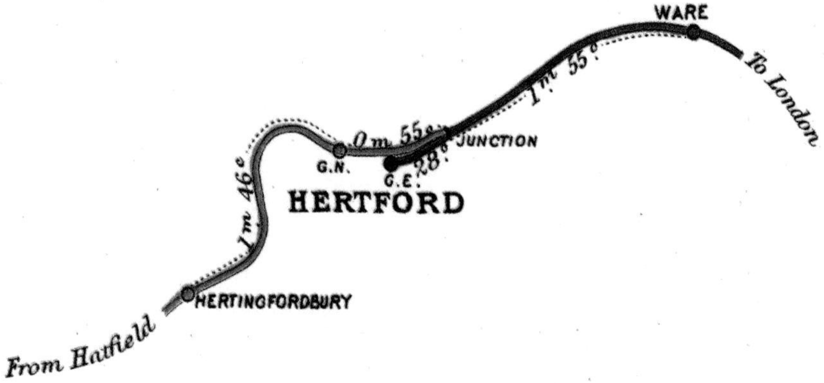

The railways of Hertford, 1914 – Railway Clearing House.*

The first portion completed was from Dunstable to Luton, opened to goods on 5 April 1858 and passengers on 3 May, initially run by the LNWR. Both of these openings had been delayed, goods through the Dunstable LNWR Station dispute and a weak bridge, and passengers due to the BoT's Leighton turntable stipulation (p.71). The opening day was manic – so many attended (many without tickets) that people clung to the train's roof and some passengers had to walk back, there being no space left for them. Unfortunately, raising subscriptions had proved challenging and company funds were overstretched. Pausing land purchase for the Welwyn section, the LNWR was approached for financial assistance in return for a lease but turned it down (although they too offered to run the completed line). Looking for a solution the LDWJR turned to the Hertford company proposing amalgamation, pooling resources and raising new capital. Despite opposition fearing greater power to the ECR or LNWR over the GNR this was passed on 28 June 1858, creating the 'Hertford, Luton & Dunstable Railway'. An unexpected consequence, however, was the GNR – unsuccessful at securing an exclusive lease – forcing tight restrictions on the linking bridge (to be a single arch built with no main line interruptions), effectively blocking its construction.

Newly revitalised, by January 1859 construction had restarted, although further delays warranted an extension to the Act. After two specials for officials and shareholders the Welwyn-Luton portion opened on 1 September 1860, LNWR operation passing over to the GNR. However, just before opening there was a major complication. On 19 April 1860 the new company ended the 1858 running agreement with the GNR and ECR (also ending their 1852 Hertford truce). In debt, a takeover was necessary, and with the sudden risk of both LNWR and ECR incursion into their territory the GNR immediately stepped up. After lengthy negotiations the lines became part of the GNR on 12 June 1861. The 1860 opening day also saw a physical change to the Hertford line. Originally terminating at Welwyn Junction (opened 1858), this was closed with trains from both branches joining the main line to terminate at Hatfield. This would in turn be amended in 1868 with the junction removed and construction of independent 3-mile tracks running parallel either side of the main line from each branch into Hatfield.

♦ *Tracks to Hertford*

Life thereafter became largely uneventful on the Hertford branch. Forced to remain an isolated track, there was no significant local development and traffic never met expectations. With only three daily trains by 1895, in 1904 railcars were trialled to attract more passengers, serving two new halts. Not frequented by other trains, these were so unsuccessful that they closed in July 1905 (Attimore Hall halt remaining for goods until 1964). The railcars were experimental Daimler petrol units maintained by GNR apprentice Oliver Bulleid, later famously of the 'Southern Railway' (SR). Services grew, however, with 13 trains by 1910.

The 1920s would see major competition, not just from local buses but from the GNR itself. Begun in 1898 the 'Hertford Loop' placed the town on a direct main line, and when opened to passengers the branch was effectively made obsolete. The new Hertford North Station opened on 2 June 1924 serving both main line and branch (as terminus), the former Cowbridge Station (itself briefly renamed 'Hertford North' in 1923) closing the same day. Ironically Hertford North was further away from the town centre than its predecessor. Cowbridge

An N7 and 'Craven' DMU meet at Hertford North Station, 1959 – B. Brooksbank.*

became a goods depot, its replacement having no such facilities, so although most London traffic was lost the branch clung to this surviving function. Passenger traffic was still supported by the LNER, lingering hopes of suburban expansion meaning there were still nine trains daily by 1939. During WWII the branch was reconnected to the main line at Welwyn, trains thereafter terminating at Welwyn Garden City.

♦ *The Line to Luton*

Early years on the Dunstable-Welwyn line were successful, particularly as the sole link to Luton's major straw plait and hat industry. Passenger services varied, incorporating a Luton-Dunstable shuttle (nicknamed the 'Skimpot Flyer' after a nearby farm), services over the full line, and some through trains to Kings Cross. By 1864 there were six trains daily plus a Sunday service terminating at Church Street from 1866 – the LNWR station being closed. There were also excursions, from Harpenden horse racing to an 1886 trip to Llandudno departing at 4:40am…

The monopoly was not to last. The MR's London extension opened in 1868, a second Luton station built alongside the GNR's, and with this main line the branch lost a primary function. But although there was an initial drop in traffic the impact was not as great as feared, competition being surprisingly little. The MR was quicker for London commuting but poorly-suited for local traffic, many preferring the better service via Hatfield. Passenger traffic still grew, with

4F No. 44414 on the Cobbler *railtour, Luton Bute Street Station, 1964 – Lamberhurst Collection*.*

ten Dunstable-Hatfield and seven Dunstable-Luton services daily by the 1890s (including LNWR-operated Luton trains from 1881) compared to 13 MR services. Demonstrating the continued use of the GNR post-MR, it was the latter's Chiltern Green Station – barely 600 yards away from Luton Hoo Station – that closed in 1952 as passenger traffic favoured the other.

Goods became highly important: while the eastern end was largely rural, from the 1870s the branch helped encourage industry around Luton, notably 'Vauxhall' motors and 'Laporte' chemicals. Improving access to cheap coal, straw plait and raw materials along with aiding national distribution helped the hat business in particular, business booming with whole trains for hats – complete with dedicated 'hat vans'. Hatting diminished with WWI but other industries flourished with most goods traffic centring on Luton-Dunstable. There was also a munitions works during WWI served by Chaul End Halt, a short-lived private facility closed in 1919. Further down the line agriculture was more central, particularly market gardening and animals. Several nurseries around Wheathampstead used imported London manure, some purportedly coming from London Zoo, with complaints from residents living by the sidings!

As with the Hertford line the 1920s was a time of change. Welwyn Garden City was founded by Sir Ebenezer Howard in 1920 and temporary halts were built on both lines close to the former Welwyn Junction to aid construction. On 16 August 1920 the Luton line platform opened to the public as Welwyn Garden City Halt (the Hertford line platform closing after construction ended), but this subsequently closed with a new LNER main line station (also serving the branch) opened on 20 September 1926. A formal opening on 5 October was undertaken by Neville Chamberlain.

By the 1930s passenger traffic had begun declining, services reducing to seven Dunstable-Hatfield and three Dunstable-Luton trains during WWII. Contrary to other branches there were no new Luton-Dunstable halts opened despite active suburban growth in the area. Goods remained important especially for the War effort (particularly from 'Vauxhall') – much being moved by rail.

♦ *The Routes*

The 7-mile Hertford line curved from Hatfield and Welwyn eastwards in a winding route to Hertford. A single track with no substantial gradients or civil engineering, the intermediate stations after Welwyn were Attimore Hall and Hatfield Hyde halts (both 1904-5), Hertingfordbury (1858) and Cole Green (1858). The half-mile GER branch connection led to their goods depot; the lack of through passenger trains meant there was no inconvenience in bypassing the GER's 1888 terminus.

The 17-mile Luton line ambled southeast through Bedfordshire and Hertfordshire in an indirect route from Dunstable to Hatfield, running parallel to the MR near Luton. A single track, there was a short 1899-built double stretch by Luton aiding goods traffic and the many private sidings in this area. Although only simple engineering, there were various gradients including a 1 in 56 at Ayot that often brought heavier trains to a stand. Intermediate

Hertingfordbury Station, 1953 – Lamberhurst Collection.*

stations were initially at Dunstable Church Street (rebuilt 1871 after a fire; 'Dunstable Town' from 1927) and Luton ('Luton Bute Street' from 1950), then once fully opened at Chaul End Halt (1914-19), New Mill End (renamed 'Luton Hoo' 1891), Harpenden ('Harpenden East' from 1950), Wheathampstead and Ayott St Peters (1877, renamed 'Ayott' and corrected to 'Ayot' both in 1878; closed 1949 after a fire).

♦ *Passengers and Problems*

Although the Hertford branch was of limited importance Cole Green Station had brief fame through filming, featuring in *When Knights Were Bold* (1936) and two episodes of *Catweazle* (1971, after closure). Most famous would be *The Lady with a Lamp* (1951), filmed just before closing and featuring LMR locomotive *Lion* (star of the Ealing comedy *The Titfield Thunderbolt*).

Such was the interest when the line from Luton opened that many locals walked to Ayot simply to experience a ride back. Amazed that '*it could go backwards as well as forwards*', one yokel declared '*Now I woon't* [sic] *believe but what they're a lot o'little ponies underneath*'. Passengers varied considerably over the years, most famous being author George Bernard Shaw, a frequent traveller from Wheathampstead. Often late, staff would hold the train for him; at Christmas they received a collective 30-shilling tip. The rail-served rubbish dump, however, led to frequent complaints with Shaw describing a smell like '*Stromboli and Hell*'! Another regular traveller, on being approached by a new inspector, declared '*my face is my ticket*', to which the inspector retorted '*my instructions are to punch all tickets!*' Animals also caused trouble, from the bored Dunstable GNR omnibus horse that wandered along its route leaving its driver at the station, to a Luton guard's sandwiches stolen from his brake van by an adventurous cat...

Arguably the strangest service offered was in the 1950s, when winter snow blocked the line. Stranded at Welwyn Garden City with roads equally impassable, refreshment was brought from a local pub and everyone slept on the train. There were also numerous accidents for such a provincial line. On 19 January 1875 a stalled coal train rolled back into an approaching passenger train. The collision knocked the engine down an embankment, but luckily there were no fatalities. An engine blowback on 20 April 1955 was less fortunate, the fireman fatally injured jumping from the cab. More amusingly, during the General Strike a stationmaster and inexperienced driver forgot to set catch-points at Wheathampstead, leading to crowds gathering around an engine leaning drunkenly atop the embankment! Then there was the failed attempt in 1898 by staff to lift a derailed tender with their bare hands... Lastly, though tangential, it was a 'Laporte' chemical truck from Luton that caught fire causing the infamous 1944 Soham Explosion.

♦ *Nationalisation and Decline*

Damaged by the 'Hertford Loop' and worsened with growing road competition, Welwyn-Hertford passenger traffic continued to fall. LNER perseverance did not continue under BR, by 1950 running five daily trains, and it was inevitable that these would cease. On 18 June 1951 the final passenger service departed, some attendees dressing in Victorian clothes. Two further railtours visited in 1959 and 1961. Goods traffic remained viable at first, but itself decreased until general goods was withdrawn in 1962, Cole Green and Hertingfordbury closing outright. Cowbridge, having been further downgraded to a coal depot, closed on 18 April 1966 along with the ex-GER link. Since c.1935 London rubbish trains served the Holywell Hyde landfill near Cole Green, this becoming the line's last function. The branch officially closed on 23 May 1966 but trains still continued. While most of the track was lifted in 1967 a short section remained at Welwyn serving two factories near the former Attimore Hall halt. This remained in use until the line's final train on 12 November 1981.

The Luton line conversely retained passengers with nine daily trains post-WWII and seven by the 1950s. By 1955 there were two Luton-Dunstable trains daily (plus two from Leighton) and eight to Welwyn Garden City (five from Dunstable and one continuing to Kings Cross). Unfortunately 1960s road growth changed its fortunes, the short Luton-Dunstable distance being deemed uneconomic even with dieselisation. It was included in the Beeching Report and earmarked for closure, objections from local councillors creating only a temporary reprieve. The final passenger train, with wreath and headboard emblazoned 'The Last Skimpot Flyer', departed on 24 April 1965; services ceased two days later. The loss of Dunstable Town Station in particular would be immortalised in the 1963 Flanders & Swann song *Slow Train*.

Goods continued but concentrated at the far ends; Ayot, Harpenden East and Luton Hoo closing in 1963, Wheathampstead in 1965. In 1966 a connection was made between the branch and MR in Luton (authorised in 1863!), rendering the line eastwards to Wheathampstead obsolete. This central part was closed the same day, lifted shortly after. The Welwyn-Wheathampstead end remained operational with 'Dustcart Special' rubbish trains to Blackbridge landfill (former gravel pits) until 24 May 1971. At the other end, Dunstable Town Station had already ceased goods in favour of the ex-LNWR goods yard, but this too closed on 9 October 1967 – general goods trains ending on 26 June. Traffic thereafter focussed on a cement works and oil depot until 30 April 1989. Mothballed, this final section officially closed in 1991. Having had many railtours, the *Chiltern Chariot* of 1987 would be the last. Luton Bute Street was all but demolished by

1968 but track remained until 1992; the last surviving track in Dunstable was only lifted in 2010.

♦ *Restoration and Reuse*

Today the Hertford branch forms part of the *Cole Green Way* cyclepath and the *Lea Valley Walk*. Much was redeveloped near Welwyn and little infrastructure remains, although platforms survive at Cole Green and Hertingfordbury Station is now a private residence. The former GNR-GER connection had been mooted for reopening but is instead being considered for another cyclepath.

The southern end of the Welwyn-Dunstable line forms part of two trails: Luton Hoo-Harpenden is another part of the *Lea Valley Walk*, and Ayot St Peter-Wheathampstead is now the *Ayot Greenway* cyclepath. Much of Wheathampstead Station was demolished but the surviving platform section has been restored as a community area. Luton Hoo Station is now a private residence. There have been long-standing calls to reopen the Luton-Dunstable stretch, almost undertaken but ended with Privatisation. There had equally been plans for a heritage railway, but with some parts redeveloped a much-contested guided busway was opened instead on 25 September 2013. With trains unlikely to return, today Dunstable has the questionable record of being one of Britain's largest towns with no rail connection, bringing things back to the original Stephenson situation of the 1840s...

The LNWR Watford-Euston DC Line

Until the 1900s the LNWR had largely overlooked suburban services, only changing with London expansion matched by a burgeoning popular desire for a suburban lifestyle. Triggering development of several lines around London, the northernmost was a purpose-built passenger electric line into Hertfordshire – the first in the Chilterns. Its use of direct current (unlike the WCML) led to its name: the *DC Line*.

The DC Line viaduct at Bushey – D. Begley.

♦ *New Ideas*

The capacity of any main line is finite, and although the WCML had been quadrupled the growing demand nonetheless led to congestion. Identifying a suburban market, wishing to free up their primary routes and with the 1906 opening of the underground *Bakerloo Line*, a project was devised to create a series of interconnected electric suburban railways. The 'New Lines' project was the largest integrated suburban network of its day, taking advantage of the LNWR's financial strength (unlike that of other companies). Gaining an Act in 1907, in 1909 they took over the Broad Street-Stratford 'North London Railway', adding this to the project. In total the venture planned electrified routes from:

- Watford Junction to Euston via a new dedicated track
- Broad Street to Richmond (crossing the *DC Line* at Willesden Junction)
- Rickmansworth branch modifications including electrification, a south-bound *DC Line* connection, an electric train depot and an additional branch to Croxley Green (p.102).

Plus services from:

- The *Bakerloo Line* to Watford Junction via Queens Park Station
- Broad Street to Watford Junction
- Broad Street to Kew Bridge
- Willesden Junction to Earls Court

Construction began in 1909, sections opening piecemeal with the first *DC Line* train (albeit steam-hauled) on 15 June 1912. This was from a temporary main line junction at Kensal Green to Harrow, the remainder to Watford opening on 10 February 1913. WWI significantly slowed development: May 1915 saw the *Bakerloo* extended to Queens Park, their trains thereafter continuing to Willesden, but electricity only reached Watford on 16 April 1917. This allowed *Bakerloo* and Broad Street services (the Richmond and Kew sections completed in 1916) but Euston-bound remained steam-only until junction modifications and a new Primrose Hill tunnel were completed. It was thus on 10 July 1922 that the *DC Line* was finally complete, electric trains running unhindered to Euston. Ironically the LNWR gained little from their efforts, becoming part of the LMS barely five months after the *DC Line's* completion.

♦ *The Route*

Mostly following the WCML southeast towards Euston, aside from connections at Watford and Camden its 16 miles operated wholly independently. At Bushey it diverged from the WCML across the Colne Valley via a 17-arch viaduct before joining the appropriated (and doubled) ex-Rickmansworth branch. Currently serving 19 stations, intermediates in the region are Watford High Street (ex-Rickmansworth branch), Bushey (WCML; enlarged 1912) and Carpenders Park (1914; temporarily closed 1917-19).

♦ *Stock and Specials*

DC Line operation would lead to distinctive rolling stock. Starting with steam, new 0-6-2T LNWR suburban engines were nicknamed 'Watford Tanks' due to their proclivity. As 'New Line' electrification progressed the first four EMUs, tested in 1914 at Earl's Court, used Siemens equipment. Sufficiently successful to warrant a further order WWI, however, stymied interaction with a German company! Instead, the electrics was sourced from the Swiss Maschinenfabrik Oerlikon. Delivered in 1915 and 1922 these 'Oerlikon units' (and LMS derivatives) became the mainstay of 'New Line' routes, working until 1963. *Bakerloo* services also used new trains, co-funded with the LNWR. Delayed by WWI, this 1920 'Watford Joint Stock' was purpose-designed for underground and main line operation, but their manual doors delayed station departures (also once causing a fatality). With questionable reliability they were replaced with 'Standard Stock' in 1930, a purpose-built batch being known as 'Watford Replacement Stock'.

After WWII Southern Region trains would travel to Wembley for an annual hockey game, the empty stock continuing northwards to Watford carriage shed. The engine would then use the triangular Rickmansworth branch junction to turn before its return, the *DC Line* consequently entertaining unusual motive

Class 378 No. 378231 flanking the WCML at Bushey – Author.

Class 313 No. 31312 at Watford Junction, 2010 – Author.

power including ex-SR Battle of Britain Class members. Fitted with both third and fourth rail power the line was also usable by other third-rail stock, helping in emergencies when diverting main line trains such as sleeper services after the 1996 Watford Rail Disaster. Specials using ex-SR EMUs similarly took advantage of the system in 1970 and 1986, running from London Victoria and Brighton to Watford Junction and Croxley Green.

♦ *From LMS to TFL*

With an initial half-hourly Watford-Euston service (higher at peak times), plus *Bakerloo* and other trains slotted between these, its success called for increased frequency. To enable this the manual signalling was replaced with an automated system in 1933, reducing the headway between trains to just two minutes. Peaking in the 1930-50s, the line offered a train every 2.5 minutes: five Euston-Watford and seven Broad Street-Watford per hour plus *Bakerloo* services. Circumstances would change though. During WWII first class was removed and by the 1960s it was suffering major decline with diminishing demand exacerbated by competition through WCML electrification. Now loss-making, both Euston-Watford and Broad Street-Watford service amendments were in the Beeching Report, by the mid-1970s decreasing to every 20 minutes off-peak

(Euston-Watford) and half-hourly at peak times (so fitting in the surviving Broad Street services). The all-day *Bakerloo* service was cut in 1965 to six per rush-hour, later just four. By the 1970s the four-rail electric system (as on the Underground) was converted to BR's three-rail system, the *Bakerloo*'s fourth rail retained where required but bonded to the third.

Reductions continued in the 1980s. *Bakerloo* trains ceased serving Watford, instead terminating at Stonebridge Park from 1982, although extended back to Harrow & Wealdstone in 1984. The reopening of London's Dalston-Stratford track signalled the end for Broad Street Station, the final Watford-bound train departing on 27 June 1986. A service continued from Liverpool Street, but this too ceased in 1992. Under 'Network SouthEast', part of their 'North London Lines', there was an unsuccessful rebranding as the *Harlequin Line* (a hybrid of Harlesden and Queen's Park station names) and in 1988 reduced train frequency allowed conversion to standardised signalling. Post-Privatisation there were thoughts of reinstating *Bakerloo* services to Watford, but with the competing MET 'Croxley Rail Link' (p.105) it was instead taken over by TFL in 2007 as part of 'London Overground'. Upgraded, Watford-Euston services operate every fifteen minutes, the line remaining a significant London commuter route.

III: Branch Lines

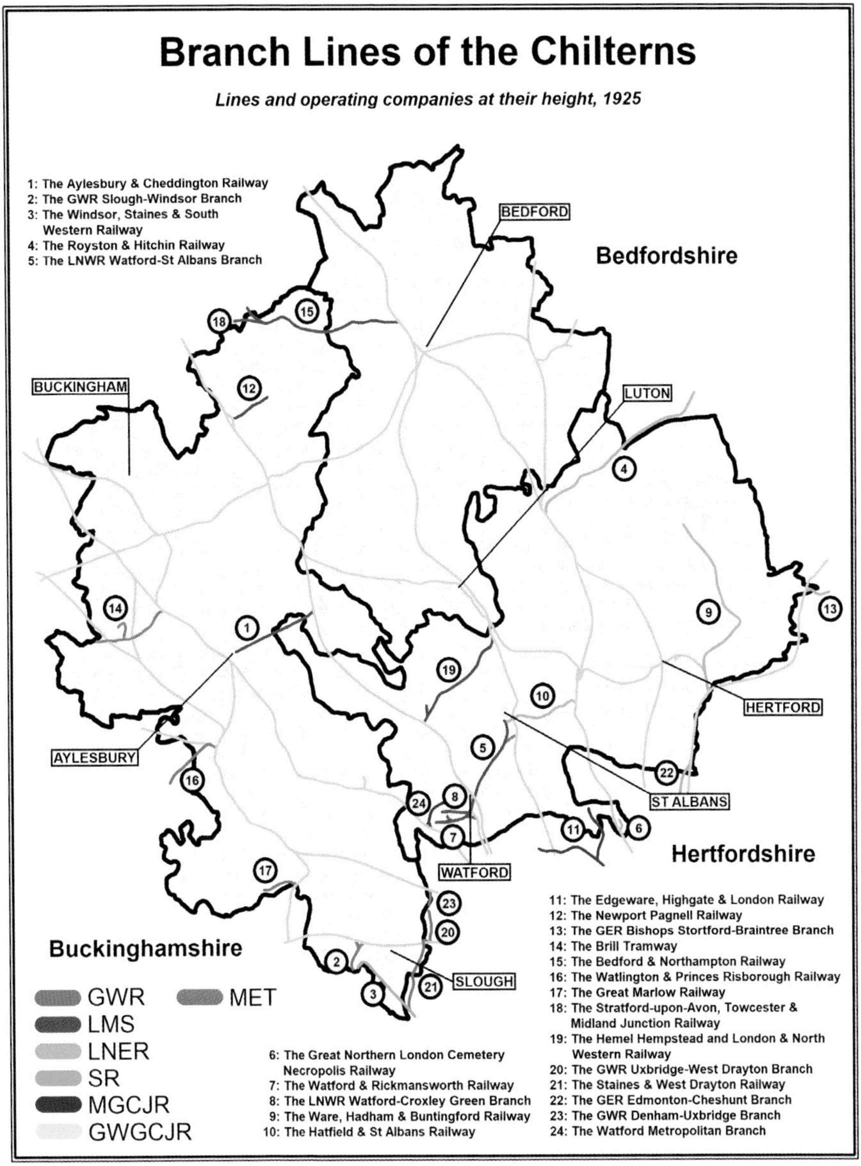

The sleepy branch line is a traditional rural scene that would famously disappear under Dr Beeching's infamous 1963 'Axe'. Whereas main lines provided a 'trunk' route, it was these small provincial lines that fed custom to them, equally reflecting the 'Railway Manias' when every settlement wanted a connection. Their histories often reveal support from larger companies, few being independently profitable hence their ultimate decline. Nonetheless they gave valuable service, many being fondly remembered decades after disappearing. While most succumbed some examples remain operational today – a reminder of their role in the community.

The Aylesbury & Cheddington Railway

Aylesbury was long a significant agricultural centre, eclipsing Buckingham as the county town of Buckinghamshire. Transporting produce was vital, building a GJC link in 1814 and similarly desiring a rail link with the nearby LBR. At a time when many still feared the new technology this forward thinking would unwittingly make it the origin of an internationally-used railway form: the world's first branch line.

♦ *From Genesis to Grouping*

On 10 November 1835 a meeting was held at the White Hart Inn. Promoted by local figures such as Sir Harry Verney, and attended by Robert Stephenson, the 'Aylesbury Railway' was formed. The original ambition was a main line running from the LBR via Aylesbury to Oxford, primarily focussing on goods traffic. After lengthy discussion authorisation for the first section to Aylesbury was granted in 1836. However, a major problem arose the following January when the local bank failed. This was worsened further when £2,000 was stolen by the bank's auditor! Losing a key supporter the ensuing panic led to a drop in

Aylesbury High Street Station on its final day, 2 February 1953 – B. Brooksbank.*

subscriptions, the project only surviving by abandoning the Oxford extension. These caused delays, as did Parliamentary discussions over a competing line to Cheltenham, plus negotiations with the LBR over a working arrangement. It is telling of the newness of rail technology that the LBR initially considered running the line akin to the canals, with independent hauliers paying tolls to run their own trains. This was swiftly rejected though when realising the problems it could cause for reliability on the main line.

Construction began in 1838 under the auspices of Stephenson. A Directors special ran on 27 May 1839, the line officially opening on 10 June with a public holiday. Speeches at a banquet included a prediction of future local branches (met with laughter) and a summary of the timesaving now possible:

> *'Prior to the railway opening the only means of travelling to London had been by coach which left Aylesbury at six o'clock in the morning arriving in London at ten o'clock in the evening, 14 hours travelling. By use of the Aylesbury Railway this will now be two hours.'*

Leasing the line in 1840 for five years, the newly-formed LNWR purchased it outright in 1846. By then the line had proved a success and continued to prosper. Passenger services rose from three trains daily to 11 by 1887, meeting London trains and some even continuing to Tring. In the first six months alone some 19,565 passengers were carried. Two local stagecoach firms tried to compete with lower fares but were forced to close. Although not as much as hoped goods traffic was substantial, serving the local dairy, brewery and printers amongst others, by the 1900s also the 'Nestlé' factory (a notable WWI traffic source). Agricultural produce was similarly important, such as the ubiquitous Aylesbury Duck. Less popular was the in-bound 'London sweepings' – horse manure fertiliser from London's streets...

♦ *The Route*

Crossing Buckinghamshire from Cheddinton to Aylesbury – the centre of the line flitting briefly into Hertfordshire – the 7-mile single track reveals the original terminus-terminus business operation of the earliest railways. Ignoring any potential intermediate connections the branch was dead straight nearly its entire route, and largely level there was no major civil engineering. Originally only serving Aylesbury Station ('Aylesbury High Street' from 1950), a stopping point at Marston crossing opened in 1857, tickets sold by the crossing-keep, becoming Marston Gate Station in 1863.

♦ *Life on the Line*

Much of the branch's daily life was quiet, but occasionally there was cause for excitement. On 12 July 1883 the branch received royal patronage when Edward, Prince of Wales visited Waddesdon Manor, home of Baron Ferdinand de Rothschild. While locals bedecked the streets, the LNWR only saw fit to ensure the station was in 'neat and polished condition'. Conversely there were occasional accidents; derailments in 1842 and 1852 each suffered a fatality, while

Coal Tank No. 58887 departs Aylesbury High Street, 1953 – B. Brooksbank.*

Webb '5ft6in' No. 46601 at Cheddington, 1953 – B. Brooksbank.*

a porter-cum-pointsman named Downes caused a mess in 1873. Changing some points under a train, derailing two carriages, his report concluded:

> *'I am very sorry it has occurred, but I will be more careful in future.'*

Most amusing though was an unexpected chase down the line. On 3 July 1843 a goods train was waiting at Aylesbury without its crew. Unfortunately the tender brake was released and the regulator not fully closed, so the unmanned train sauntered off by itself. While another locomotive followed in hot pursuit the runaway demolished a level crossing gate before reaching Cheddington, where it joined the main line and continued to Leighton Buzzard before running out of steam!

♦ *Decline and Closure*

With growing traffic the LNWR looked to expand Aylesbury Station, but the site was too cramped. A new passenger terminus consequently opened on the High Street on 16 June 1889, the former station made a goods depot. As with its predecessor there was no platform run-round loop forcing the use of gravity shunting, rolling coaches back into the station for the engine to rejoin. This only ended in 1950 with the introduction of push-pull trains. Traffic was not the sole consideration behind station location though. By 1870 the WR and ABR had reached Aylesbury, from 1892 served by the MET, giving more convenient alternatives. In spite of reducing branch travel times London traffic was lost and the line began to decline; under the LMS services from 1937 diminished to nine trains daily. WWII depressed numbers further, some being wary after the line was struck by two bombs. With ever-decreasing importance, after Nationalisation service numbers shrank further – at its lowest, winter 1952-3, having just four trains daily (none with London connections).

On 31 January 1953 the last passenger train departed amid cheers and detonators, the service being formally suspended two days later. Goods continued, particularly coal to Aylesbury gasworks and agricultural machinery from the 'New Holland' factory, but road haulage spelled the end. On 2 December 1963 the line was closed outright with the tracks lifted by mid-1965. Disappearing a year before Beeching's Report, ironically it was the superseded canal that survived into preservation. In spite of its historical significance, little remains today. Much of the trackbed forms field borders, while Marston Gate Station is a heavily-rebuilt private residence. Disappearing back into the countryside, it is a shame there is little recognition for so important a railway.

Railway Rivalries – the two Windsor Branches

In the late 1840s the southern tip of Buckinghamshire was crossed by two branch lines to Windsor, one barely within the county's borders. While only relatively minor lines with little mileage, their joint histories reveal the lengths that Victorian companies went to when competing with each other and encroaching on their so-dubbed 'territories'.

Windsor & Eton Riverside Station – G. Sheppard.*

♦ *The Windsor, Staines & South Western Railway*

First put to Parliament in 1847, this small company's initial aim was a railway linking Staines, Windsor and Slough (the latter historically part of Buckinghamshire). The proposal lay close to both the GWR and 'London & South Western Railway' (LSWR), so both companies began vying for the Windsor connection – not merely for royal prestige but equally for the significant passenger and goods traffic that followed Queen Victoria when in residence. With Parliament and the company granting support to the LSWR it would appear the GWR had lost out. The Staines-Datchet section opened in August 1848, connecting to the LSWR Richmond line. Construction continued towards Windsor, Prince Albert personally supervising the survey through Windsor Home Park, but delays in agreeing access caused the full line to only be completed a year later, opening on 1 December 1849. In 1848 before even finished the LSWR had taken it over from the erstwhile company, however, circumstances had already changed the line's prospects dramatically.

♦ *The GWR Slough-Windsor Branch*

After Parliament favoured the LSWR, rejecting any potential takeover, the GWR took a different approach. In 1848, in blatant competition, they proposed

In the shadow of the Castle: Windsor & Eton Riverside, 1990 – S. McKay.*

their own branch to Windsor from Slough. But as with the main line (and a failed 1833 branch proposal) there was a significant opponent. Eton College feared the railway could endanger their students both physically and morally (affecting discipline and enabling wayward travel), and while they failed to prevent the line they did gain financial compensation, force a deviation around Eton High Street and the College, block any station being built serving Eton directly and make the GWR employ a watchman to ensure the safety of students. Barely 2 miles long, the broad gauge line was rapidly constructed and featured a Brunel-designed 'bowstring' bridge over the Thames (a forerunner of his Saltash Bridge in Cornwall), today claimed to be the oldest regularly-used wrought iron railway bridge in the world. The finished line was opened on 8 October 1849 – seven weeks before the LSWR branch. Windsor thus gained two railways in the space of two months, blocking any monopoly and limiting each other's potential profitability from the very start.

Brunel's Thames bridge at Windsor – C. Allen.*

♦ *Consequences and Continuation*

With both lines complete Queen Victoria had the option of routes – LSWR for the Isle of Wight or GWR to London for Sandringham and the north. Conversion of the GWR branch to dual gauge in 1862 made royal travel even easier, no longer needing to change trains when breaking gauge. The lines also benefitted from Windsor Castle opening to visitors in 1845, giving tourists easier access from London. Unfortunately in 1882 the GWR station was also the site of Victoria's eighth assassination attempt...

The intended LSWR extension from Windsor to Slough was abandoned, although two further stations outside Buckinghamshire were added. Such was the rush to completion that the original Windsor & Eton Riverside Station was only temporary, the proper station with royal facilities being completed in May 1851. With an LSWR line from Staines to Wokingham built in 1853, the line became part of the SR in 1923 and was electrified in 1930. Temporary connections to the former 'Staines & West Drayton Railway' (p.135) were installed during WWII and the 1980s, while the branch gained its own sub-line c.1890s-1960s when a three-quarter-mile spur was built supplying a Staines pumping station.

The GWR branch saw various changes since opening. The original wooden Eton Viaduct was rebuilt in brick in the 1860s, while Windsor Station (renamed 'Windsor & Eton' in 1904 and 'Windsor & Eton Central' from 1949) was heavily rebuilt for Queen Victoria's 1897 Diamond Jubilee. Plans for an extension to Ascot in 1871 ultimately stalled though through opposition – including from the LSWR. From 1863 the line was also briefly used by MET trains and in the

1880s by the 'Metropolitan District Railway', the tracks altered in 1883 to standard gauge only. Although with no intermediate stations a short-lived exception existed at Chalvey Halt c.1929-30. The western arm of the triangle junction at Slough, previously only used for excursions, Royal Trains and storage, was closed and lifted in 1964. Goods traffic ceased around the same time and the line was reduced to a single track, the terminus similarly diminished.

Windsor & Eton Station, 1977 – G. Skelsey.*

Today the two Windsor branches remain operational, testament to the competition between companies during the 'Manias' and still reflected in the current franchises: 'Great Western Railway' and 'South Western Railway'. Plans for their future have been regularly discussed, from a new link to Heathrow to connecting the two termini, but for now they are likely to continue largely as they have since opening.

The Royston and Hitchin Railway

By the 1840s and the second 'Mania' public fears had disappeared, proposals multiplying exponentially. Between civic pride and company wrangling duplication became rife – especially to important and lucrative locations. Well sought-after, Cambridge was already on the 1845 ECR main line but this did not prevent interest from the GNR...

◆ *Competitive Origins*

Several companies had considered an Oxford–Cambridge line, ultimately achieved by the LNWR (p.45). In 1846 a proposal by the 'Cambridge and Oxford Railway' was slashed by Parliament, only permitting the Hertfordshire section between Royston and Hitchin (on the GNR main line). Duly renamed the 'Royston & Hitchin Railway' (RHR) it was immediately supported by the GNR, both for potential access to Cambridge and – just as significantly – to prevent the ECR backing the proposal so entering GNR 'territory'. Under this support the GNR guaranteed shareholders 6% on paid-up capital, and in 1847 leased the branch even though still incomplete. Enthusiastic to reach Cambridge an extension was proposed that year, rejected, and another applied in 1848. This succeeded in authorising track from Royston to Shepreth – a strategic location. Around the same time the ECR was developing a line of their own, from Cambridge to Bedford. This only led to a single track branch from their main line at Shelford (just south of Cambridge) to Shepreth. Consequently the GNR's extension reached a line straight into Cambridge, but successful operation as a through route hinged on the relationship between the two companies.

On 21 October 1850 the Royston-Hitchin branch opened, the Shepreth extension being completed on 1 August 1851. The ECR branch, conversely only opened on 1 April 1852, delayed through quarrelling (blocking attempts at a separate GNR Cambridge terminus) and likely further aggravated by the Act declaring that should ECR construction be delayed then permission would transfer to the RHR. Meanwhile the Royston line was found to be increasingly constrained – a short agricultural branch costing the GNR nearly £15,000 annually because of the shareholder guarantee. They even ran a horse omnibus service from Shepreth to Cambridge, which despite undercutting ECR fares was only short-lived. However, the GNR had a way out. In February 1852 an agreement between the rivals was formed: the ECR would lease the GNR branch for fourteen years, running trains from Hitchin to Cambridge. Operationally the line became known as the Shelford & Hitchin Railway, running three trains daily (later four). Through services to Kings Cross were provided by joining coaches to London-bound GNR trains.

♦ *The Route*

Running 12.75 miles the terrain forced several gradients, but limited civil engineering kept costs down even with double track demanded by the Act. Intermediate stations after Hitchin were at Letchworth Garden City (a 1903 halt made official in 1905; named 'Letchworth' 1937-99), Baldock and Ashwell ('Ashwell & Morden' from 1920). The 5-mile extension from Royston to Shepreth included a steep 1 in 100 gradient and Meldreth Station (Cambridgeshire) reaching the end-on 'Shepreth Branch Junction' linking to the 5.25-mile ECR

Ashwell & Morden Station, 1992 – B. Brooksbank.*

Shelford line. In spite of being one physical track, administratively it remained two separate branches.

♦ *Changing Powers*

During the lease the ECR was often behind with payments, the company's finances always strained, and this continued under the 1862 GER. Meanwhile the GNR began reconsidering the Cambridge link via a potential post-lease takeover of the RHR, the ECR obstructing by refusing access to their main line. This changed with the 1862 opening of the LNWR-worked BCR (p.51). As the GNR and LNWR were friendly, the GNR proposed to either cooperate with the ECR – using their metals, doubling the single-track Shepreth branch and sharing their Cambridge station (with a separate GNR terminus considered) – or to build a new line from Shepreth to the LNWR line and enter Cambridge from there. Seeing how this would render their branch useless, the ECR complied and an agreement was made on 2 May 1864. Operation returned to the GNR on 1 April 1866, by when the modifications were meant to have been completed. However, problems arose.

A newly-introduced Class 101 DMU at Baldock, April 1961 – B. Brooksbank.*

In preparation for the changeover, a joint inspection of the line was made in 1865, revealing that the cash-strapped GER had let it deteriorate. Worse still, there were insufficient sleepers used, so the GNR's engineer insisted on the replacement/addition of 11,400 sleepers. These were supplied on time but not fitted, the GNR having to finish the work. Before this could be completed, on 3 July 1866 sleepers 'in the last stage of rottenness' caused a derailment injuring nine passengers and killing the footplate crew. The GER Shepreth branch was in no better condition, also suffering a derailment that year, and with insufficient finances the track doubling and station modifications were incomplete. Ultimately the GNR had to loan the GER £5,000 to finish the work, accomplished by May 1867.

With this complete the GNR had their Cambridge link and the dual-branches underwent a rare transformation: with some through services from Kings Cross, it became a main line. Inter-company competition remained intense, pushing speeds to reduce timings, but superior GER acceleration forced the GNR to focus instead on developing traffic en-route rather than just terminus-terminus business. Having remained an independent company throughout, on 1 July 1897 the RHR was finally absorbed into the GNR, by 1898 having six trains daily.

Letchworth Station, 2000 – B. Brooksbank.*

♦ *Letchworth*

Once an agricultural branch, now part of a main line to Cambridge, the line would also gain a notable destination of its own. Having first proposed theoretical pre-planned new towns in 1898, in 1903 Sir Ebenezer Howard envisioned Letchworth as the site of a major social experiment: the world's first 'garden city'. Railways were vital to the plan, and the GNR created Letchworth Garden City Halt that year to assist in construction. Intended for workers and visitors, it was only officially opened to passengers on 15 April 1905, gaining a railmotor service between Hitchin and Baldock and in 1913 a full Arts and Crafts-style station. Passenger and goods traffic grew significantly by the 1960s, Letchworth cementing the value of the line.

♦ *The LNER and Onwards*

From 1923 the GNR and GER both came under the LNER, although the two Cambridge routes continued their rivalry. The two branches were finally considered a single line, boosted by residential and industrial growth around Letchworth, Baldock and Royston.

In May 1932 daily *Garden Cities Express* services were introduced, soon renamed the *Cambridge Buffet Express*. Highly popular, the three-coach trains occasionally had to be extended to ten coaches, and while suspended with WWII they were reintroduced in December 1948. Traffic remained high under BR, the line ultimately overtaking the ex-GER main line as the primary Cambridge route, and in 1978 as part of a wider programme it was electrified up to Royston. Running thrice-hourly services (seven at peak time), it connected with diesels to Cambridge but as such ended the through express. It was only under 'Network SouthEast', and with the completion of ex-GER main line electrification, that this was extended from Royston to Cambridge, completed on 16 May 1988. Passing through franchises after Privatisation, 'Govia Thameslink' began operations in 2014. Far removed from its lowly origins, today it continues to be a valuable commuter and express line.

The LNWR Watford-St Albans Branch

St Albans is one of Hertfordshire's leading settlements, a city from 1877, and it would gain several rail connections. The first was a line now popularly known as the 'Abbey Flyer', built directly by a national company rather than absorbing a local concern. Surviving later challenges, it remains a picturesque and useful community asset.

♦ *The Early Years*

Despite its significance St Albans had been bypassed by the LBR and its residents were keen to get a connection. A failed 1840s ECR plan triggered LNWR interest and, intending a route through St Albans to Uxbridge, an Act was passed in 1847. Unfortunately, a national economic crisis led to it being abandoned, the notion only reinvestigated after the opening of the GNR main line. Planning a route to Amersham, Parliament granted the LNWR assent in 1853 but just

Experimental AVC Railcars Nos. 1-3 at St Albans Abbey Station, c.1952 – T.H. Watts.

for the Watford-St Albans section. Some considered that they merely intended to block GNR expansion, construction being heavily delayed, but this may have equally been due to debates on Watford Junction (Lord Ebury criticising existing provisions and thoughts of demolition in preference of Bushey Station). Furthermore, the intended terminus was on the site of the Roman city of Verulamium and landowner Lord Verulam complained, so the end 1.5 miles was abandoned, instead terminating at the bottom of Holywell Hill. After requests from the Council construction finally began in 1856, although slowed by poor weather and ultimately reduced to a single track to save funds.

Opened on 5 May 1858 there was a public holiday, former Mayor John Lewis declaring '...the railway would be of a very great advantage to all'. Not all were apparently keen though – on 9 March a test train carrying dignitaries including Robert Stephenson was nearly derailed after bricks were 'wickedly placed on the line'. The railway certainly had a major impact. While the LBR had dented stagecoaching,

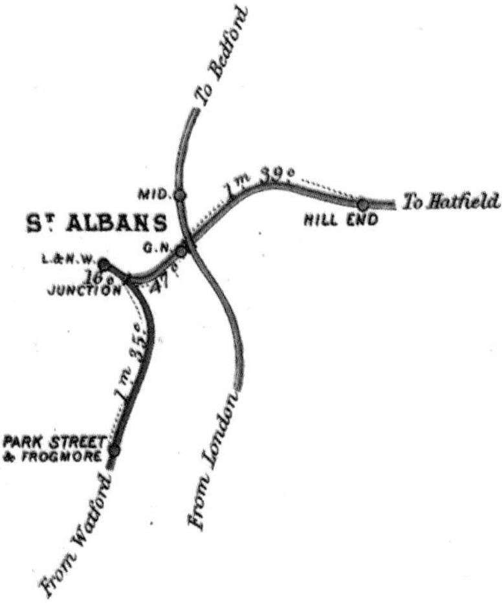

The railways of St Albans, 1914 – Railway Clearing House.*

the branch decimated it and many supporting inns went bankrupt. Originally there were six trains daily, many through to Euston, although London traffic only grew in importance by the 1870s. The completion of the MML through St Albans in 1868, however, prevented the branch from really growing, even with a connection to the GNR Hatfield branch in 1866 (p.108). Goods traffic began on 7 May 1858, becoming notable for coal, building supplies and general merchandise. Private sidings also developed serving north Watford printing firms. By 1889 there were 14 trains daily.

1888 saw the start of improvements, particularly at Bricket Wood which by 1900 had grown as a tourist attraction with fair. Coincidentally, here in 1904 engineer George Flooks opened Britain's first public miniature railway. During WWI the line saw use transporting local army volunteers plus many horses to a Royal Army Veterinary Corps site set up near St Albans Station. With the Grouping the line fell under the LMS and by WWII there were 30 trains daily. Goods increased as industry expanded, particularly around Watford North Station, while St Albans gasworks remained important for coal traffic.

Bricket Wood Station, 1947 – T.H. Watts.

♦ *The Route*

The 6.5-mile track travels northeast from Watford Junction plotting an obstacle-free route, bar some minor gradients and two large cuttings, into St Albans Station (renamed 'St Albans Abbey' in 1924 to differentiate it from the ex-MR station). Originally there were just two intermediate halts, Bricket Wood (temporarily closed 1859-61) and Park Street & Frogmore (briefly closed 1858; renamed 'Park Street' 1974), but the line later gained Callowland (1910, renamed 'Watford North' 1927), Garston (1966) and How Wood (1988, to coincide with electrification). There was also a sub-branch connecting to the MR main line, built in the 1860s to aid the latter's construction and closed c.1883-98. Alongside the 'Croxley Rail Link' (p.105), this was briefly considered for reopening by BR, linking the MET, WCML and MML.

♦ *Movies and Near-Misses*

The branch hosted various railtours in the 1950-60s but most unusually LMR locomotive *Lion* visited in 1937 for the filming of *Victoria the Great*, a siding at Bricket Wood dressed to represent Paddington! Other films included *Double Confession* (1950), *Up the Creek* (1958) and *She'll Have to Go* (1962). Diesel

Class 321 No. 321416 at St Albans Abbey, 2011 – Author.

experiments began in 1934, continuing in 1952 with an ACV Railcar set nicknamed the 'Flying Brick', but regular DMU usage only commenced in the 1960s. Using assorted units, this variety often led to unusual destination boards – once even listing Blaenau Ffestiniog! Today the 'Bricket Wood Station Heritage Trust' is preserving the station building, but nearby is another historic structure. In 1954 an 'Air Raid Precaution Railway Control Centre' was constructed: a Cold War bunker as an emergency operations base in case Euston was incapacitated.

In February 1976 a repeat of Stephenson's near-miss occurred, when vandals blocked the track with timber and concrete near St Albans. A local cyclist managed to flag the train down with his bike lamp just in time. BR wrote to thank him, though reminding him that he should not have been cycling along the trackbed. Later it was found the bicycle had been stolen... The line's sole notable accident occurred on 12 February 1988 when a DMU arriving at St Albans Abbey failed to stop, overshooting the terminus by 45 feet. Fortunately, no-one was injured.

◆ *From Beeching to Today*

The 1951 closure of the connected GNR line did little to damage the branch, by then still running 27 trains daily alongside three dedicated goods services. But 1960s decline, dropping to one-engine operation, saw the line appear in the Beeching Report as a potential cut. Goods ceased in 1964, but it was saved by housing expansion on the route near Watford, instead gaining Garston Station. There were problems from 1974 with the diesel-run branch meeting the newly-electrified WCML, plus the 1971 gasworks closure, but services remained faster than local buses. Then running 22 daily trains, the October 1975 cessation of Sunday services met with protests, forcing their reinstatement in December and giving a slight boost to passenger numbers. BR subsequently supported the line, refusing to truncate it in 1983 when threatened by the M25 motorway, and after further housing development electrified the route, completed on 11 July 1988.

In 1989 under 'Network Southeast' there was talk of closing the St Albans terminus as part of the potential ex-MR link reopening. Heavily opposed, this triggered the formation of a local action group. Subsequently named 'ABFLY' it became a key component of the line's post-2005 'Community Rail Partnership' programme and continues to have direct involvement with operations. After passing through post-Privatisation franchises, in 2017 the LNWR returned in the modern guise of 'London Northwestern Railway'. With discussions of development and service expansion, prospects look good for this branch survivor's future.

The Great Northern London Cemetery Necropolis Railway

Growing Victorian urban populations coupled to high mortality rates created mounting problems with burials, especially within London. Several projects aimed to resolve the issue, most famously the Waterloo-Brookwood Cemetery London Necropolis Railway, but this was not the sole UK example.

In the 1850s the 'Colney Hatch Company' purchased land in Barnet (then Hertfordshire) for a new cemetery, located just north of Colney Hatch Station (Enfield; today 'New Southgate Station') on the GNR. Intending foremost to cater for poorer individuals, an agreement was formed with the GNR creating the 'Great Northern London Cemetery Company'. This oversaw specialist funeral trains transporting coffins and mourners from a dedicated sub-station at Kings Cross 7 miles away. At its destination trains diverted off the main line onto a short spur serving a private station within the cemetery. This included a neo-gothic station building flanked by a chapel and cemetery superintendent's house.

Easily the smallest complete Chiltern 'branch', barely a mile long, it was also the shortest-lived. The service commenced in 1861 but was highly unprofitable with limited demand. This was probably not only due to the comparatively short distance between the cemetery and London (roads therefore a viable and cheaper alternative) but also most burials being of paupers with few mourners. Using a bespoke 'coffin carriage', fares (separate from interment costs) were subdivided by class, offering mourners single or return and a set six-shilling rate for the coffin (single). No single or third class tickets were ever sold. Free tickets were offered for those wishing to inspect the cemetery and Sunday trains established to suit the working hours of poorer clients, but even so the company had to request reduced operating rates from the GNR. By 1863 the service had diminished to essentially only when required, and that April it was suspended outright. The agreement between the companies formally ended in 1865, although some final cemetery-bound trains (terminating at Colney Hatch) ran after the cholera outbreak of 1866

Today nothing remains of the railway. The Kings Cross sub-station wa demolished in 1962, the spur line sold to the GNR and lifted in 1888, while the cemetery station building was demolished c.1912-14. The last surviving trace was the nearby 'up line' signalbox, demolished in 1973. Having nothing to do with the branch itself, instead being named after the area's main landmark (actually outlasting it by two years), it retained the ominous name 'Cemetery'...

The LNWR Rickmansworth and Croxley Green Branches

These two Hertfordshire branches, partially sharing tracks, had an interconnected history of unfulfilled hopes. Impacted by MET competition, its partial takeover by the Euston *DC Line* (p.82), however, gave it retrospective importance as a step towards that vital modern commuter route.

♦ *The Watford & Rickmansworth Railway*

The idea of Lord Ebury of Moor Park, Hertfordshire, the 'Watford & Rickmansworth Railway' was part of his grand vision for a north London orbital railway. Intended to meet the GWR Uxbridge branch (p.135), linking Watford and Paddington, initial GWR support was withdrawn and Parliamentary permission never granted. Instead only a short branch was built, nicknamed the 'Ebury Line', to the small pre-Metroland town of Rickmansworth.

With the Directors almost all local landowners, Ebury as Chairman, work was initially rapid. Plans were made public in March 1860, assent granted on 3 July, and the first sod cut on 22 November. Ironically that day Ebury declared that 'the day's ceremony was of little importance if only a line from Rickmansworth to Watford was built'... Construction slowed with financial difficulties (and three failed inceptions), opening with little ceremony on 1 October 1862. Originally there were six trains daily, operated by the LNWR, plus experiments using railmotors and in 1870-1 a St Albans through service. Passenger numbers were good, notably schoolboys and Saturday Watford Football Club matches, while goods was similarly significant with watercress to Watford Market. Company finances, however, remained questionable and several private sidings were constructed in the 1880-90s, notably to 'Benskins Brewery' and Dickinson's paper mill. Although many hoped the line would encourage Rickmansworth's economy it ultimately had the reverse effect, drawing business away towards the ever-expanding Watford.

The closed Rickmansworth Church Street Station, 1972 – D. Hillas.*

All but bankrupt in spite of these efforts, the company was absorbed by the LNWR on 27 June 1881, becoming part of their 1907 'New Lines' project. Alongside building the *DC Line* (appropriating and doubling part of the branch) this included electrification of the Rickmansworth track, formation of a triangle at the Rickmansworth *DC Line* junction by adding a west-east track to Bushey Station (enabling London-bound branch trains), a new electric train depot and a new branch to Croxley Green.

♦ *Expansion to Croxley Green*

Mirroring the Victorian 'Manias', the early twentieth century saw growing competition for suburban railways. The LNWR and MET were keenly aware of the potential surrounding Croxley; the LNWR plan was largely devised to counter future MET competition, the Watford MET branch already slowly developing (p.139). While the LNWR jested about the MET branch heading for an area called 'The Wilderness', their Manager Robert Selbie retorted:

> *'If you saw Croxley Green* [LNWR Station] *today you would see it standing like a pelican in the wilderness, at least half a mile from Croxley Green village and serving nobody.'*

Its open rurality certainly supported, if inadvertently, the LNWR's motto 'Live in the Country'...

Construction began in 1908, passenger services commencing on 15 June 1912. Although to be an electric line initial services were steam, often railmotors as passengers were limited. Goods traffic began that October, and the Bushey link track opened on 10 February 1913 with the complete (but still steam-hauled) *DC Line*, enabling direct albeit infrequent Croxley-London services. On 10 March 1913 Croxley Green Station had the ignominy of being razed to the ground by arson, the work of Suffragettes who purportedly asked a policeman for directions...! Croxley Depot opened on 16 April 1917, first used by Watford *Bakerloo* trains (later also *DC Line* and branch stock). It was only on 30 October 1922 that the Croxley branch commenced an electric service, following completion of *DC Line* electrification in July. From then there were c.30 trains daily to various destinations.

♦ *The Routes*

The 4.5-mile branch passed from Watford Junction through Watford High Street Station (originally the sole intermediate stop) before curving southwest to Rickmansworth (renamed 'Rickmansworth Church Street' in 1950 to distinguish it from the MET station). A canal bridge was the route's sole major engineering feature, while later interchange sidings at Rickmansworth Station took advantage of the neighbouring GJC Batchworth Lock.

With the Croxley branch's construction and impending *DC Line* use, Watford High Street Station was enlarged c.1912 with double track. After this shared section the Croxley route diverged westwards just south of the Rickmansworth-Bushey junction – also the location of Croxley Depot and the triangular link towards London. Intermediate stations were at Watford Stadium (1982) and Watford West (briefly named 'Hagden Lane'; temporarily closed 1914-18.

♦ *Rickmansworth After The Grouping*

Rickmansworth became the last of the 'New Lines' electrified, finally completed under the LMS on 26 September 1927. This delay was no doubt connected to the branch's diminishing fortunes: passenger traffic falling away with growing competition from buses and the newly-opened Watford MET branch. The limited housing expansion around its Croxley and Rickmansworth Stations compared to the burgeoning Metroland must have further exacerbated the issue. Unfortunately with electrification the branches discovered a significant issue. Initially they used LNWR Oerlikon units, but demand on the local sub-station proved so excessive that these caused voltage drops. Consequently c.1930-39 (after which Oerlikons returned) they received lower-voltage ex-*DC Line* 'Watford Joint Stock' tube trains just withdrawn from the *Bakerloo*-Watford service.

A Class 508 at Watford High Street Station (now the Watford-Euston DC Line), 2007 – Dr N. Clifton.*

Even with electricity the branch failed to recover, from 1931 trains being third class only and never gaining a direct London service. Unsustainable, passenger services ceased on 2 March 1952, the last train carrying around a dozen enthusiasts and only a single genuine passenger. Goods continued though, gaining a new siding serving 'Goodyear Tyres' in 1955 but losing others such as to 'Benskins Brewery' in the 1960s. Closed in 1967, one had even served a 1932 narrow gauge line to the 'Colne Valley Water' pumping station at Eastbury. The branch closed outright on 2 January 1967, track lifted the following year, but even then there was a partial stay of execution. The spur to Croxley paper mill was still required for oil deliveries so the truncated branch continued in operation until finally closing on 20 January 1983. Purportedly the final factor in ceasing operation was the single-line token being lost, floating away down river…

♦ *Croxley's BR Days*

During WWII services to Croxley diminished, those to London largely ceasing by the end of the War. The branch was included in the Beeching Report, but

An Oerlikon unit developed for the LNWR 'New Lines' – Author's Collection.

while the Bushey link was shut in 1966 Croxley retained passenger operations. Contrary to other branches it was goods that ended first, on 14 November 1966. Croxley Depot had been demoted to a stabling point c.1965, used by *Bakerloo* trains until 1982 and closing in 1985.

4 December 1982 witnessed an unusual modern branch event: the opening of a new station. Watford Stadium Halt was funded by partners including Watford Football Club, being opened by Club Chairman Elton John. Built expressly to serve the football grounds at Vicarage Road it only operated for home events, while its intention of separating unruly fans in the town centre gave rise to the nickname of 'Hooligan Halt'. This did not herald a resurgence though, nor did a short-lived 1988 'Network SouthEast' rebranding as part of the *Harlequin Line*.

Watford West Station, 1985 – M. McDonald.*

As the branch became increasingly run-down, facilities demolished, an increased twice-hourly service in 1988 was the line's final chance. Failing, from May 1993 only a single 6:00am train kept running. As with the Victorians, costly permission was required to close a railway and it was found cheaper to run a token Parliamentary 'ghost train'. This continued until March 1996 when a new access road severed the terminus, but even with a 160-foot gap in the track it was only in 2003 that the mothballed branch was finally closed.

♦ *Relics Today*

Nothing remains of Rickmansworth Church Street Station, lost to a housing estate. Much of the trackbed up to the Croxley line junction, however, survives as the *Ebury Way* cyclepath, its name recognising the line's main supporter. Most of the Croxley line survives in an abandoned state, long-standing intentions being to connect it to

Croxley Green Station, 1984 – B. Brooksbank.*

the Watford MET branch, bypassing both termini but enabling underground trains to run direct from Baker Street to Watford Junction. First suggested after WWII and reinvestigated in the 1990s and 2010s, the 'Croxley Rail Link' has endured repeated setbacks, most recently being cancelled in 2018. Nonetheless, discussions continue and the line quietly waits in hope of future trains.

The derelict Watford West Station – Author.

The Ware, Hadham & Buntingford Railway

Buntingford in Hertfordshire has been a notable market town for generations, but when bypassed by the ECR its prospects were threatened – compounded by rail-instigated stagecoach decline. Despite optimistic plans for a rail connection circumstances meant the branch constructed was ultimately only minor. Even so, 'The Bunt' was a valuable local link, remaining a fondly-remembered institution.

♦ *Early Challenges*

On 1 August 1856 George Mickley proposed a railway to 150 landowners at a special meeting at the *George and Dragon* Hotel. Anticipating a 5% profit, no local opposition was found and authorisation for the 'Ware, Hadham & Buntingford Railway' (WHBR) was granted in 1858. Led by engineer Henry Palfrey Stephenson, a founder of the Society of Engineers, work commenced in 1859 near Westmill with a ceremony marking cutting the first sod. The tented banquet was drenched with rain – an inauspicious start. Things would not improve. Poor response to shares caused financial difficulties, while unexpected landowner issues increased costs through compensation. Worse still, opposition meant that despite the company's name it could no longer join the ECR at Ware. Instead, in 1861 Parliament approved a deviation with the branch now commencing at St Margarets (also on the ECR Hertford line; p.65). With finances already tight the Directors considered mortgaging the incomplete line, but no one was prepared to take the shares for this.

Competition would be its saving grace. The GNR Hertford branch lay nearby (p.75), and the risk of a GNR takeover spurred the ECR into giving assistance. £22,000 was granted to the WHBR, with two ECR board members joining the company and the ECR to work the line. This support enabled the railway's completion and on 10 February 1863 a special director's train ran to Buntingford

Braughing Station, 1961 – B. Brooksbank.*

direct from London. That April the line was inspected by the BoT ready for opening. It did not go well. The track was deemed substandard, the signalling incomplete, fencing inadequate and more. One bridge near Braughing even sank 3 inches under the weight of the train, requiring rebuilding. Another was found to have used low-grade timber, being life-expired by only 1868. These corrections were a costly delay, forcing another Act to raise further funds. Inspected again in June permission was reluctantly granted and on 3 July 1863 the line opened, celebrated with a banquet. Four trains originally ran daily and there were around 30,000 passengers in the first six months – a reasonable success. Goods traffic was far less, not least as facilities were minimal.

An ex-GER N7-3 at Buntingford Station, 1959 – B. Brooksbank.*

The ECR merged into the GER in 1862, but its relationship with the WHBR deteriorated – the cash-strapped operator considering its 50% receipt share insufficient for the work involved and funds invested. Itself bordering on insolvency, in 1865 the WHBR asked the GER for a takeover, admitting they could not pay any dividend. The issue led to the company going before the Court of Chancery in 1866, investor Walter Bentinck being awarded £3,039 'payable in land if not in cash'. The WHBR had neither, only being resolved when the GER settled on their behalf. By then the GER realised the line's future again hinged on them and, still conscious of the risk of GNR incursion, in 1867 they proposed absorption. Taken over on 1 September 1868, track improvements were made following a derailment and Widford Station was closed. Though underused a local petition challenged the decision, it reopening three months later. As commuting grew in the area the branch began to thrive – Mardock, Widford and Westmill being elevated from request stops to full stations. With strengthened revenue the line could be improved, some stations being rebuilt. Goods traffic also grew, notably agricultural such as from the rail-connected Standon flour mill. By 1900 there were seven daily trains plus three goods services; from 1901 through services began to Liverpool Street and by 1915 it peaked at 11 trains daily.

♦ *The Route*

The 14-mile line travelled north from St Margarets Station (Hertford branch), with stations at Mardock, Widford, Hadham, Standon (rebuilt 1869 following a fire), Braughing and Westmill before reaching Buntingford. This demonstrated hopes of potential extension, being designed as a through station. Much had steep gradients, peaking at 1 in 63 near Hadham, and although little major civil engineering was required expense came from the unusual number of bridges – crossing the rivers Ash and Rib eight times.

♦ *Criminals and Celebrities*

The area's rural nature meant stations were often somewhat remote. Braughing Station suffered as a result in 1890 with a spate of six break-ins, each increasingly brazen. One time a lit candle was placed in the window to illuminate the booking office, making it easier to search – open parcels found scattered about. Later the Stationmaster's waistcoat, coat and his gold pencil case were pilfered, while on another occasion the miscreant subsequently broke into a platelayer's hut and cooked himself supper with fish stolen from a parcel! No-one, however, was ever caught...

Braughing saw happier times – and more reputable visitors – with the 1953 filming of *Happy Ever After*, starring David Niven and Yvonne De Carlo. Other films were also produced on the line, such as *Operation Bullshine* (1959) with Donald Sinden and *Postman's Knock* (1962) with Spike Milligan.

♦ *The 'Big Four' to Beeching*

The growth of commuting with residential expansion by the 1920s became almost an LNER equivalent of Metroland, reflected in cheap tickets and promoting its scenery to encourage walkers. But with rising London passengers this success had a counterpoint. Goods traffic had already fallen to a single service and the rise of buses weakened local traffic. Economies ensued and although London-Buntingford through trains grew (one way; Buntingford-London trains only commencing in 1939), a general rail strike in 1924 lost some passengers for good. During WWII there were frequent ordnance trains to a depot near Buntingford, often under Home Guard protection, plus some evacuee specials. Services briefly halted in 1945, however, after a V2 rocket struck near Hadham. After the War nature became the line's opponent, with winter flooding at Braughing in 1947 and snowdrifts in 1958. Goods traffic similarly suffered with a local outbreak of foot and mouth disease in 1950.

By the mid-1950s and growing car ownership passenger levels began falling again – it was easier for commuters to drive directly to main lines rather than change trains. Through trains ended in 1959 (just before 1960 Hertford branch electrification), and steam was replaced with DMUs. With decreasing off-peak services (nine daily by 1960) and hoped-for branch residential expansion not developing, the Beeching Report listed it for closure. Locals objected, proposals arising for a cheaper railbus instead, but nonetheless the line closed to passengers on 16 November 1964, the last DMU departing two days earlier. Goods continued to Hadham,

N7-3 No. 69688 at St Margarets Station, 1959 – B. Brooksbank.*

Standon and Buntingford, but this too ended on 17 September 1965. Four months later the track was lifted bar a short spur at St Margarets, serving a gravel pit until March 1969. Today portions of the trackbed are footpaths, part also used in the A10 road. Buntingford and Braughing Stations survive as private housing, Braughing sporting an ex-BR carriage. Sadly the remainder is gone, but even so with its own historical society the branch continues in local memory.

The Hatfield & St Albans Railway

St Albans gained a rail connection with the LNWR in 1858, but other companies had previously declared interest. An 1845 ECR proposal under George Hudson (which inspired the LNWR's scheme) had been blocked by the GNR, who in turn considered their own connection as part of their growing web of branches. Their idea, however, was to lead to financial ruin, creating a distinct example of the sharp practices surrounding early rail development.

♦ *An Unsteady Start*

In 1846 a GNR line to Dunstable was planned. Permission was granted for the Hatfield-St Albans section but despite St Albans Corporation pleas the project was dropped to concentrate on their London-York main line. By the 1860s two thirds of their St Albans traffic had been lost to the LNWR branch, spurring the GNR into action. Without sufficient spare capital of its own they sought to encourage a local company – probably well in the knowledge of its potential failure.

The 'Hatfield & St Albans Railway' (HStAR) was formed by local landowners, notably Lord Ebury (of the Rickmansworth branch) and the Hon Reginald Algernon Capel (of Cassiobury, Watford). Parliamentary approval was granted in 1862 for two lines: the branch itself and a secondary spur near Hatfield that was ultimately not built. Connecting to the LNWR branch (p.96), running powers were given to the GNR into St Albans Abbey Station, and vice versa for the LNWR to London Road Station. While the GNR contributed financially most funds proved challenging to raise, much via loans. Then in 1863 the MR applied to Parliament for their St Pancras extension, to pass literally yards from the HStAR. Construction of the branch had not yet commenced, but in spite of the obvious danger it nonetheless went ahead.

The restored Nast Hyde Halt on the 'Alban Way' – M. Izzard.

On 16 October 1865 the HStAR opened, the first train bedecked with flowers but elsewise with little ceremony. Operated by the GNR, the contract optimistically declared that the line, in good maintenance, should be returned to the HStAR after a 999-year lease: AD2861. Services originally comprised eight trains daily terminating at London Road, from 1 November 1866 continuing on weekdays through to the LNWR station. Company rivalries meant issues arose though, LNWR staff hindering purchase of GNR through tickets. As London Road was a little way out of town a dedicated omnibus was introduced, but this fell foul of Lord Verulam. The London Road turnpike gate lay between the town and station, and despite lengthy arguments Verulam refused to move it. Until the gate's abolition in 1871 the HStAR consequently had to pay £10 annually to enable the omnibus and other necessary vehicles to pass unimpeded.

Revenue was never exceptional, and with reports by 1867 of a 'prevailing distrust in railway securities' after the third 'Mania' the company bore ever-increasing loan interest. By 1866 services had decreased to seven trains although this improved to ten by 1882. It was too late. In 1868 the MR St Pancras extension opened and the HStAR was ruined: traffic fell and debts could not be repaid. Despite further GNR loans by 1870 the company was insolvent, but there was a further bitter irony. In 1866 the GNR had offered to purchase the branch; against the Directors' advice the shareholders refused. In 1867 the Directors tried to reopen talks, to no avail. Acutely aware of their 'present [financial] embarrassment', a secret meeting held with the GNR in 1882 alarmed the shareholders but, now bankrupt, there was little alternative and the GNR again offered a buy-out. Taking over on 1 November 1883 the GNR now had the branch they wanted, but even with their earlier financial contributions they paid over £40,000 less than it had originally cost to build...

The MR at St Albans c.1880; the HStAR London Road Station visible centre left – Author's Collection.

The surviving London Road Station – Author.

Competition with the MR for London traffic was severe, and despite some short-lived through trains to Kings Cross it was not viable. Instead the GNR increasingly focussed on developing more successful local traffic. Several new halts and sidings were opened from 1897 but hopes of attracting new factories failed to materialise. Coal was the primary goods traffic alongside agricultural produce, also carrying substantial quantities of London manure. Back to eight daily trains by WWI, the early 1920s would prove the high point for traffic on the branch.

♦ *The Route*

Leaving St Albans Abbey Station (LNWR), the six-mile single track skirted south of the town to St Albans (London Road) Station, located right by the MR main line. Heading northeast it passed through intermediate stops at Salvation Army Halt (1897; previously called 'Sanders Siding'), Hill End (1899), Smallford (the only intermediate station when first opened; renamed from 'Springfield' in 1879 to avoid confusion with another in Scotland), Nast Hyde Halt (1910) and Lemsford Road Halt (1942). The largest of only limited civil engineering was a bridge and embankment crossing the River Ver. Private sidings served local businesses, such as the 1901 Salvation Army's Campfield printing works and Butterwick banana warehouse (previously a wartime food store). Another siding at Hill End entered the 'Hertfordshire County Mental Hospital' delivering building materials and supplies, during WWII giving access for ambulance trains.

♦ *Special Occasions*

Various trains visited the branch, from Victorian excursions aiming to boost passenger usage to railtours in 1955 and 1961 – including the first enthusiast

Nast Hyde Halt, 1963 – Lamberhurst Collection*.

Smallford Station, c.1900 – Lamberhurst Collection*.

train run by 'celebrity' GNR J13 Class No. 1247 (the first privately preserved ex-BR locomotive, then based at Hatfield). The most important was in 1889, a rare through train via the LNWR when the Shah of Persia (the guest of Lord Salisbury PM) travelled from Hatfield to Berkhamstead non-stop via the two branches. Another key event was the 1896 'Bath and West and Southern Counties' agricultural show held near London Road Station. Many of the displays came via the line, the disused second platform used for disembarking animals.

The line featured in films, notably *Rookery Nook* (1930) and the 1970s *The Return of the Saint* and *The Rivals of Sherlock Holmes*. Later operations seem to have had an unofficially relaxed attitude, a Nast Hyde farmer often offering the driver rabbits if they stopped for him at the lineside, while one driver purportedly used to bring a shotgun to score pheasants from the cab! Less positively, in August 1955 vandals meddling with points caused the morning goods train from Hatfield to detour into Sanders Siding, smashing the buffers and ending up on a footpath with four derailed wagons behind.

♦ *A Continuing Decline*

With growing road competition the 1930s saw the start of a continual decline. In 1938 a further daily service was added but with WWII the LNER economised and withdrew passenger services outright. This only lasted three months, resurgence coming from an unlikely source. The 'De Havilland' aircraft factory lay nearby, and with many commuting employees engaged in War work they wished to minimise the number of cars, lest seen by the enemy. Passenger trains thus restarted and in August 1942 a new private halt was opened at Lemsford Road (formerly Fiddle Bridge Siding) – on neither timetable nor maps. Furthermore, 'Marconi Instruments Ltd.' opened a factory at Hill End, the branch again proving beneficial to the War effort. The wartime traffic levels did not last with Peace, services being reduced again. Under BR there had been national accusations of deliberately hindering branch travel as an excuse for closures, and the decision here to delay passenger trains while the engine picked up printing works vans certainly brought complaints! Passenger numbers fell ever-farther, and as part of post-war cutbacks the last passenger train departed on 28 September 1951.

Continuing with goods but still loss-making, general goods trains ended on 5 October 1964, thereafter only fulfilling existing contracts – from 1965 the banana store becoming essentially the sole reason for continued operation. Hill End Station burned down in 1954, but with no passengers it was not rebuilt. The link track to the ex-LNWR branch was abandoned in 1964 and, with no trains beyond Smallford, the line up to Colney Lane Bridge was severed and lifted. By the end only a final contract with a scrapyard at the former Smallford yard kept the branch alive, and on 31 December 1968 trains stopped for good.

♦ *Remnants and Preservation*

Much of the trackbed is now the *Alban Way* cyclepath, opened in stages c.1985-8. Previously there were thoughts of reopening as part of a direct Watford link but, considered unviable, overbridges were removed and the Hatfield A1 motorway tunnel cut through. Remnants still survive though. Alongside London Road Station platforms remain at three halts, while the rare station building at Smallford is the focus of the 'Smallford Station & Alban Way Heritage Society'. Part of the community even long after closure, the branch's heritage and local value is set to continue well into the future.

The Edgware, Highgate & London Railway

Scarcely in the region, the 'Edgware, Highgate & London Railway' was established in 1862, intending to connect Finsbury Park to Edgware, with branches to Muswell Hill and High Barnet proposed in 1864 and 1866. Supported by the GNR (their main line connecting at Finsbury Park) they purchased the line before construction was finished, commencing services in 1867. Modifications led to trains terminating at Moorgate after 1869, partial installation of double track in 1870, an 1873 Highgate-Alexandra Palace branch and a connection to Broad Street in 1875. Further plans were proposed in the 1860s for connections to Watford, but these came to naught.

The portion built impacting Hertfordshire was the branch from Finchley Central to High Barnet Station (formerly part of the county). Opened on 1 April 1872 with intermediate stations in Middlesex, faster urban expansion in Barnet and Finchley than at Edgware resulted in this branch taking over from the original Edgeware line as the primary route. An unfortunate side effect was extreme overcrowding, the service not increasing to cope with demand and hampered further by slow goods traffic. Some passengers even resorted to purchasing their own carriage keys to lock others out further down the line! Additional stations south of Finchley Central and the rise of alternate Edwardian transport through trams and motor vehicles began to reduce the issue, however, as did expansion of the Underground network.

Becoming part of the LNER under the Grouping, the line was absorbed into the LPBT Underground network on 14 April 1940 as part of their 1935 'Northern Heights' expansion project. Numerous plans were made, notably Edgware electrification and another extension from Edgware to Bushey Heath, but WWII overtook intentions. Passenger services to Edgware ended in 1939, this section

*High Barnet Station, 2008 – M. Addison**

continuing as a goods-only line until 1964 when road transport and the decline of domestic coal use removed any remaining demand. Today sections are nature reserves. Underground stock movements continued occasionally on the Highgate-Finsbury Park portion until 1970 when it too was closed (BR having ceased goods traffic in 1964), the tracks lifted in 1972 severing the remaining High Barnet line from BR metals.

One part of the project, however, was successfully achieved. The High Barnet branch was linked to the *Northern Line* at Highgate in 1940 (simultaneously electrified), running jointly with the LNER until 1941. That year new Underground tracks and platforms were opened, the above-ground Highgate Station operating under the LNER and BR until closed in 1954. BR goods traffic continued until 1962 when High Barnet Station's good yard closed, thereafter becoming a passenger-only underground line. Today the High Barnet branch is the only remainder of these tracks still in operation: the northernmost part of the *Northern Line*.

The Newport Pagnell Railway

Located new Wolverton, Newport Pagnell (Buckinghamshire) suffered from post-LBR coaching decline, its subsequent branch line ironically succumbing in turn to 1950s roads. But during its life the 'Newport Nobby' (purportedly named after an early locomotive) would become a much-loved community asset. Not only was it invaluable for local workers but its route would have unusual origins.

♦ *An Uphill Struggle*

*Bradwell Station, 1962 – B. Brooksbank**.

In January 1817 Newport Pagnell gained a connection to the latest transport technology: a 1.25-mile canal 'arm' off the GJC. Passing through seven locks and terminating at a wharf, it carried some traffic but was not overwhelmingly successful. Its path, however, inspired later plans for a railway. Early proposals were short-lived, with limited finances and even less local support. One of 1845 under Robert Stephenson wanted to use the canal (suitably filled in) for the trackbed, but the LNWR's purchase offer was stoutly refused. Another in 1846 was described by the Duke of Bedford as 'that useless railway'; its failure was inevitable.

In 1863 Parliament authorised the 'Newport Pagnell Railway' (NPR), celebrated in the town. The LNWR supported the scheme, James McConnell of Wolverton Works noting how it would aid the workers' commute while the NPR also pointed out how much of the town's traffic was going to the rival MR. Despite objections from canal companies the canal arm was purchased and closed in 1864 when construction commenced. The first train, comprising ballast trucks filled with navvies, ran on 30 September 1865 but a proper opening would be substantially delayed. The LNWR wanted £500 annual rent for use of Wolverton Station (then at its second site) but the NPR flatly refused, the junction remaining incomplete. The contractors were also to supply initial rolling stock and staff, prolonging things further. On 8 May 1866 the BoT passed the line, bar the Wolverton junction, and to quicken proceedings the NPR agreed with the LNWR a one-third annual rent and additional £80 for the junction. The line opened to goods on 24 July 1866, taking over some of the former canal business, which was still less than expected. Repeatedly announcing – and retracting – opening to passengers many locally grew impatient, while relations with the LNWR failed to improve – the latter reporting the NPR in 1867 to the 'Railway Clearing House' for failure to pay. Finally with BoT modifications undertaken the branch opened to passengers on 2 September 1867, celebrations lasting two days with events and decorations. A free trip was offered but so many attended that most were left on the platform. The jubilation did not prevent sarcastic newspaper comments though...

The former Newport Pagnell branch trackbed (left) at Wolverton Station – Author.

The NPR, however, had grander plans. The branch was envisioned as part of a longer double-track line to Olney (Bedfordshire, later with its own line, p.124) and Wellingborough (Northamptonshire), permission being granted c.1865-6. Construction began immediately, notably a bridge at Newport Pagnell over the Wolverton Road, but things went very wrong. The previous delays coupled with LNWR obstructions and wider financial difficulties meant funds ran out, and in June 1866 work stopped. Authorisation lapsed in 1871 and the scheme was officially abandoned in 1875.

Initially running six trains daily (eight by December), nearby Stantonbury had grown as a satellite town for railway workers called 'New Bradwell', and the exploding local population meant passenger traffic was substantial. Agricultural traffic also grew, and the line even featured specials for the local steeplechase. Complaints, however, arose ranging from poor train lighting to excessive noise. Newport Pagnell Station's approach road often flooded, becoming such a quagmire that the local newspaper quipped '... if nothing is done the making of stilts will become an important local industry.'

A surviving tramcar from the 1887 Wolverton & Stony Stratford Tramway, the largest ever used in Britain – Author, with permission from Milton Keynes Museum.

In the meantime LNWR difficulties reappeared. Station rent was again questioned, the LNWR withholding through traffic revenue in response, and the NPR risked being expelled from the 'Railway Clearing House'. The NPR thought the treatment unfair, one director comparing it to charging entry to a shop, and costing virtually a fifth of their annual receipts they pushed for reductions. The financial situation became so severe than in 1870 the LNWR begrudgingly agreed to loan a locomotive – for a daily repayment. Worsened by the failed extension, the NPR simply could not meet its debts, so on 3 July 1873 they invited the LNWR to purchase the line. Following a detailed survey (down to the number of chairs per station) the LNWR offered either an annual rental in perpetuity or outright purchase on condition that the Olney extension be cancelled. Purchase was agreed, the LNWR taking ownership on 29 June 1875. The purchase price had included demolition of the unused extension bridge, but this was delayed until c.1879 with the arch used for storage.

Traffic remained strong, carrying nearly 600 workers daily – far more than many other branch lines. Commuting to Wolverton Works was the primary passenger movement of the area, most via the branch or Stony Stratford tram. By 1887 there were ten trains daily. The LNWR sought improvements, modifying the line to meet their new 1882 loop station, and c.1902 adding an additional spur to make the junction a turning triangle. There were even thoughts of electrification in 1904 as a test-bed, while an experimental petrol-electric railmotor visited in 1913.

♦ *The Route*

Despite purchasing the canal the 4-mile single track did not directly follow its course, the railway being more direct. Passing northeast via significant gradients of 1 in 80, most of the line comprised embankments and cuttings with a substantial lattice girder bridge over the GJC at Linford. Leaving Wolverton, intermediate stations were at Linford ('Great Linford' after 1884) and Bradwell (opened just after the branch). Bradwell had the only private siding outside of Newport Pagnell; used by a lime works and in the 1920s an oil depot, its curve frequently derailed the Ivatt Class 2 tank engine, crews becoming adept at fast re-railing. Ongoing canal competition meant no siding provision was required at Linford, potentially also reducing goods traffic on the branch as a whole. Newport Pagnell Station repurposed former canal warehouses for its yard (retaining the name of 'Old Shipley Wharf') and was designed for through running rather than as a terminus, in hopes of the aborted Olney extension.

♦ *Christmas and Complaints*

A major part of the community, the line saw various novel occurrences. There were no serious accidents, although on 1 January 1916 the shed at Newport Pagnell burned down destroying the resident locomotive. During WWII a driver, playing a prank, hid detonators in front of the engine; when moved the noise echoed in the early morning. The staff were unperturbed, until the local Home Guard advanced with rifles having heard the explosions! The largest incident was on 21 November 1959 when a passenger train overshot the platform, entered the yard and collided with stored workmen's carriages. No casualties were reported, but the damaged carriages were written off. More cheerfully, for many years Father Christmas used to attend the annual bazaar, arriving in style by rail rather than sleigh.

Having decreasing importance, many of the branch's later engines were worn out – one Coal Tank's leaky regulator meant the cylinder cocks had to remain open when stationary, permanently enveloping it in steam. Running a one-engine operation, such upkeep partially contributed to occasional illegal practices – propelling (non push-pull) trains rather than going round them at Newport Pagnell. Branch Fowler 2-6-2T No. 40043 steamed so poorly that the coaches' vacuum brakes were once disconnected and the train proceeded without them! Incongruously the junction triangle was used for turning prestigious items, this little branch consequently being frequented by the likes of No. 6229 *Duchess of Hamilton* and even the Royal Train. Railtours also visited in 1954 and 1964.

Arguably the branch's biggest single interaction with locals was rather unexpected. The line had only a poor water supply at Wolverton Station, drivers commonly using a large tank at Bradwell instead. This was supplied by a stream - as was Bradwell town itself. As house numbers expanded many found their water supply drying up whenever the engine arrived. So many housewives complained that drivers were banned from taking water on Monday washdays! The problem continued, so eventually the water column wheel had to be padlocked...

♦ *The Last Years*

Unlike road-based decline elsewhere, the branch retained passengers due to the Works and local school, although off-peak usage was falling. From 14 trains daily

Coal Tank No. 58887 on a railtour at Newport Pagnell, 1954 – B. Brooksbank.*

in 1939 it fell to nine by 1941, and with Works cutbacks in the 1950s the line grew increasingly uneconomic, having six trains by 1961. Thanks to the nearby 'Salmon & Sons' coachbuilders the line saw regular 1950s traffic transporting new Aston Martin motorcars. Strangely, at the same time the Newport Pagnell yard was still shunted by horse!

In 1963 the branch fell foul of the Beeching Report but locals fought back, an enquiry being held on 7 June 1964. Closure was confirmed in spite of the £1,400 BR deficit being relieved by a £3,000 BR-subsidised local bus (part of a £10,000 contract). Three years short of its centenary, the last train ran on 6 September 1964. Just as with the opening the community came out in force, cleaners washing the train and a bucket of water drenching a stand-in 'Dr Beeching'. So many attended that additional workmen's carriages had to be added to the train. Graffiti on a noticeboard at Bradwell declaring 'MARPLES MUST GO' reveals some recognised the real power at work: Transport Minister Ernest Marples, instigator of the Report and director of a road construction company...

Although closed to passengers, goods traffic was still proactive, albeit diminishing – a single daily train working coal and scrap services. A new coal depot was constructed at Wolverton in 1967, branch goods ceasing on 22 May and the former junction used as a siding. The line from Bradwell had already been severed on 31 December 1966, and in 1968 the track was lifted. The remaining siding survived until 1973. Today the trackbed is part of the Milton Keynes *Redway* cycle network and remnants can still be found, from the intermediate platforms to a preserved signal at Newport Pagnell. Although discussions of reopening are unlikely to succeed, with this reuse the route nonetheless continues to serve its community.

The GER Bishops Stortford-Braintree Branch

Western Essex was slower in developing a rail system, so in 1859 the ECR was contacted by local businessmen proposing a railway from Bishop's Stortford (Hertfordshire) to Braintree via Dunmow in order to more easily transport malt and barley. Connecting to another branch at Braintree, this in turn reached the ECR's other main line at Witham. Support was immediately given – not only did it increase the company's 'territory', but it also blocked an earlier competing plan, support drying up. Assent was granted in 1861, the ECR coming under the GER the following year. The project continued unchanged (despite the two terminus towns decreasingly supporting the venture) and the line opened on 22 February 1869, albeit over-budget and having failed its first BoT inspection.

Almost entirely in Essex, this line had only minimal impact on Hertfordshire with none of the nine connected stations being therein. There was little need for passenger traffic and only limited goods, but this would change in the 1880s. New industry in Braintree, coupled to increasing agricultural demand from London, led to growing goods traffic becoming the mainstay of the line. Passenger levels remained low, but even so Easton Lodge Halt (Essex) was built in 1895 at the behest of the Countess of Warwick. This enabled easier travel for her guests, the branch thus being frequented by the future Edward VII.

Bishop's Stortford Station, 1961 – B. Brooksbank.*

On the Grouping the LNER attempted to improve passenger levels with more services, but with little success. Goods was pivotal, especially during WWII with building material, munitions, and supplies for several Essex airbases. Such were their importance that trains were often strafed by the Luftwaffe. There were also ambulance trains from June 1944 to Hockerill Halt, en-route to Haymeads Lane hospital. Under BR the railway's days were numbered. Rising road competition meant trains were virtually empty, and on 1 March 1952 all passenger services were suspended. On the last day over ten times the usual number of passengers flocked for one last ride, the train having to be doubled in length. Goods traffic, particularly fruit, gave a lifeline but this was not to last. Road competition led to goods ceasing in late 1971 and, after a final enthusiast's special, the line closed completely on 27 July 1972. Today the trackbed is the *Flitch Way* cyclepath, with a visitor centre at Rayne Station. There have been various discussions about reopening the line, from the early 1970s (before the track was lifted in 1974) to a 'Campaign for Better Transport' inspection in 2019, but for now its future looks to remain as a charming countryside walk.

The Brill Tramway

Richard Plantagenet Campbell Temple-Nugent-Brydges-Chandos-Grenville, Marquess of Chandos, was the LNWR's Chairman from 1857 but resigned after his father's death in 1861. Becoming the Third Duke of Buckingham, family financial problems meant only Wotton House remained in his ownership, located near the Buckinghamshire village of Brill. The area was isolated and with the estate needing to be profitable he turned to his railway experience. Thus arose a famously eccentric line that evolved from a private tramway to the strangest branch of the MET network.

♦ *A Private Endeavour*

Having diverted the ABR towards Quainton (p.31) the Duke looked to create a small agricultural railway linking it to his estate. In 1870 under Manager Ralph Jones 20 estate labours were employed to prepare the trackbed for contractors, providing post-harvest work. As the entire route was on private land it did not require an Act of Parliament. Built cheaply and horse-drawn, Quainton Road to Wotton opened on 1 April 1871, coal from the first wagon being distributed to the poor. By November it was extended to Wood Siding. The LNWR began thrice-weekly Quainton services collecting milk and the tramway settled into operation.

Although goods-only estate employees occasionally hitched a lift, and the Duke was soon petitioned for a passenger service. In January 1872 a timetable was released for the 'Wotton Tramway': mixed passenger/goods trains twice daily. The same year the tramway was extended three quarters of a mile to a new terminus at Brill. The weight of trucks had previously been misjudged though, damaging the track, straining horses and triggering derailments, so with the new traffic Jones recommended using steam. By mid-1872 two Aveling & Porter engines (chosen for their lightness) enabled three daily trains and water tanks were installed replacing a horse-friendly pond. When the first engine arrived the horses were sold, but there was no driver, so embarrassingly the horses had to be hired back! In 1873 the Duke sought to have the tramway elevated to railway status, the BoT duly inspecting. A key requirement was a minimum speed of 12mph which could not be met, stopping places also being considered inadequate. Although permitted to continue as a tramway, the title of 'railway' remained elusive.

Passenger numbers grew but overall were somewhat sparce. Small surprise when it was quicker and cheaper to walk! Goods remained prevalent, especially coal, manure, bricks, cattle and milk, a subsidiary cartage business also developing. In November 1872 the tramway and ABR agreed to through goods, but increased coal haulage rates in 1876 spelled disaster. With road competition already developing Jones froze tramway prices – wrecking its already diminishing finances. 1874 saw a temporary boon though with the construction of Waddesdon Manor for Baron Rothschild. Completed in 1889 it produced substantial business, new engines helping counter the line's unreliable reputation, although finances remained

The preserved Brill branch platform and waiting room, Quainton Road – Author, with permission from the Buckinghamshire Railway Centre.

unsteady. Ironically the locomotives ever-increasingly concentrated on goods trains, passenger services being by horse – hired in as passenger numbers rose.

As the sole rail connection the ABR was vital to the tramway's success – the Duke also its Chairman. Unfortunately Jones and ABR Manager J.G. Rowe increasingly clashed, Rowe regarding the tramway as a nuisance. Traffic charges increased disproportionately, while ABR trains would miss connections, milk going off. Jones asked the Duke to intervene but little improved: at one meeting Jones and Rowe even nearly traded blows. Legal advice suggested the Duke would be likely to win any proceedings, but with the ABR itself financially unstable this could trigger its closure. Jones proposed a monthly £25 ABR subsidy to maintain a passenger connection; they agreed to £5. As local farmers changed from milk to beef goods traffic fell by over half. Badly weakened, even affording operational expenses became a challenge.

♦ *The Route*

The 6-mile line ran southwest from Quainton Road; a simple affair without earthworks or bridges. Gradients were shallow, albeit with brief steep sections – a winding route avoiding hills. There were seven intermediate stops before Brill: Waddesdon Road ('Waddesdon' pre-1922), Westcott, Wotton, Church Siding (closed to passengers 1894) and Wood Siding. Originally these were little more than 6-inch earth banks acting as platforms, although 1894 improvements resulted in conventional stations. There were also numerous sidings serving local needs. The 'Winchendon Branch' opened in 1876 to help building Waddesdon House, closed with completion in 1889, while another siding served the House's private gasworks c.1883-6. The most substantial was Church Siding, leading to the 1.5-mile 'Kingswood Branch' (1873-1910). Serving a coal wharf built on often-flooded ground, its location was purportedly due to an argument between the Duke and an adviser – the Duke tossed his hat on the ground and the wharf was built where it landed!

The former Brill branch trackbed – Author.

♦ *The Oxford & Aylesbury Tramroad*

Despite its precarious finances the tramway would see an unexpected renaissance. By the 1880s the MET was extending towards Aylesbury, and in 1883 the Duke announced plans to extend the tramway to Oxford, creating what would be the shortest London-Oxford route. Forming the 'Oxford, Aylesbury & Metropolitan Junction Railway', it gained assent that August. Directors included the Duke, Sir Harry Verney and Baron Rothschild, the MET also giving support. Grand schemes floundered though: despite these Directors, insufficient investment blocked advancement and in 1888 a cheaper version was authorised – just before the original Act would have expired. Renamed the 'Oxford & Aylesbury Tramroad' (OAT), this was to remain a light tramway rather than full railway. Jones, however, was reticent over its financial practicality.

Aveling & Porter No. 809 (known as Old Chainey*) on a recreated Brill train – Author, with permission from the Buckinghamshire Railway Centre.*

On 26 March 1889 the Duke died, the estate and tramway passing to his nephew, the Fourth Earl Temple. Verney died on 12 February 1894: two key supporters now gone. As MET expansion developed in the 1890s the OAT extension stagnated. Its Act was lengthened in 1892 and a deviation bill prepared in 1894; electrification was also considered. On 1 April 1894 a clause in the 1888 Act was enacted and the tramway subsumed into the newer company. Jones remained as manager and work began upgrading the existing track and stations. Quainton was similarly rebuilt by the MET in 1897 with better tramway access. Further new locomotives reduced journey times from an hour to 35-43 minutes, four services running daily from 1895. Nonetheless passenger levels remained poor and Earl Temple frequently had to give financial support. Predictably, the Oxford extension plans came to naught.

♦ *Mishaps Galore...*

With such a peculiar line there inevitably were unusual occurrences. On 26 August 1871 a London excursion was arranged from Wood Siding. Carrying 150 people, horses drew coaches to Quainton and locomotives thereon to Aylesbury, where they were attached to a GWR service. The experiment was never repeated: tree branches on the wooded tramway endangered passengers, the weather was poor, and delays at Slough meant the return train only finally reached Wood Siding at 2:00 am. In later years reliability improved but the branch retained a slower pace. On one occasion the train stopped before a station and the engine uncoupled for shunting, only for staff to discover there was still a passenger on board – they had been forgotten about!

As limited funds led to decreasing maintenance, accidents became a normality. 1872-3 in particular saw several instances including an entire goods train derailing, a locomotive's drive chain breaking, the funnel snapping off, and the flywheel coming loose – shooting down the line only just missing a flagman! Things improved over time but with occasional exceptions: c.1929 a lone van rolled away from Quainton, demolished a crossing gate and almost reached Waddesdon before slowly rolling back again down the gradient. Despite these, low speed meant there was a good safety record with only one fatal incident. On 8 March 1883 three ladies' maids from Wotton House were walking along the track near Church Siding. An approaching train whistled, but Maria Nicholls failed to clear the track, being struck and killed.

♦ *The Brill Branch*

With the ABR absorbed into the MET and London through trains from 1897, on 27 November 1899 the MET leased the tramway. From 1 December they took over operations, retaining Jones, and it became their Brill Branch. Track weight restrictions remained, forcing the purchase of the existing rolling stock, inspection safety concerns emphasised by derailments of 1903-introduced ex-ABR D Class engines. Re-laid in 1910 the BoT authorised a speed of 25mph and, now capable of handling larger engines (electrification also creating surplus steam traction), venerable 1860s MET A Class 4-4-0Ts were introduced. Although

MET No.23, formerly of the Brill branch – Author, with permission from the London Transport Museum.

older than any previous tramway stock they were also strangely the most technologically advanced. Having worked the line since opening Jones retired in 1903, operation now fully under MET control.

Meanwhile the GCR had been marching towards London. Its construction had boosted traffic of building materials, and in 1906 the branch became part of the new MGCJR. The subsequent GWGCJR and Aynho line similarly provided construction traffic, both crossing the tramway, but on completion offered a faster alternative. The GWGCJR's Wotton Station was so close to the branch's own that they later shared a stationmaster. The line now had real competition and suffered accordingly. Brill was a centre for cadet training in WWI, providing some passengers, but by the 1920s and rising road usage the OAT grew desperate to sell. Despite repeated attempts to several companies, all declined.

Coming under the 1933 LPBT this sleepy rural branch surreally became part of the ultra-modern *London Transport* network – although 50 miles away from central London. Traffic was very thin, the line losing c.£4,000 annually, and some trains ran without a single passenger. Maintenance diminished and derailments repeatedly ensued. Preceding the 1936 end of MET services north of Aylesbury, in 1935 the Brill branch became its first cut. After a rushed inspection closure was confirmed, the last passenger train departing on 30 November. Saluted by fog detonators and singing, the packed train was trailed by enthusiasts in cars.

A final train ran that evening, collecting station documents and valuables, and at midnight the track was ceremonially severed from the MET. Reverting to the OAT, whose purpose had become simply collecting the annual rent, the lack of funds or rolling stock prevented continued operation so in 1936 everything was sold piecemeal and by 1940 the company was wound up.

♦ *Remnants Today*

Much of the line today is gone, just thicker roadside verges and the occasional building, with part between Quainton and Waddesdon forming the *Tramway Walk* footpath. But at Quainton, now home of the 'Buckinghamshire Railway Centre' (p.33), the tramway platform and waiting room survive in active use as a demonstration line and exhibition. There were thoughts of reopening a section, but as it stands at least part of this iconic branch still echoes with steam.

The Bedford & Northampton Railway

Originating in 1845 with the aim of crossing Bedfordshire, Buckinghamshire and Northamptonshire, the 'Bedford & Northampton Railway' (BNR) was the third company to attempt the route, granted an Act in 1865. This authorised five railways but only two were constructed: Bedford to Northampton and a junction to the 'Northampton & Peterborough Railway'. Even with this reduced plan construction was significantly delayed – the Act extended twice – and a planned dedicated Bedford terminus was replaced by running into the MR Bedford St John Station. Built under Charles Liddell with tight curves and steep gradients this was only ever intended as a slow branch line, with stations at Turvey (Bedfordshire), Olney (Buckinghamshire) and Piddington (Northamptonshire) leading to the Northampton St John's terminus. The MR agreed to operate the line, likely in part to compete with the LNWR around Northampton, ultimately taking it over in 1885.

Olney Station with a Bedford-Northampton service, 1962 – Lamberhurst Collection.*

The railway opened on 10 June 1872 but celebrations were delayed until July due to the death of the Duke of Bedford. Barring some special trains to the Towcester Racecourse passenger traffic was never substantial; the initial five daily trains rose to seven by 1938. Stations were remote and served no major communities, probably contributing to the 1939 LMS decision to close the Northampton station, instead using the ex-LNWR's. Local goods was reasonable (plus through trains), WWII aiding growth with Piddington benefitting from Yardley Chase MoD depot.

In the 1950s BR tried to encourage passengers, considering a new Buckinghamshire halt (unbuilt) and in 1958 introducing diesel railcars on a nine-train service. The line nonetheless stagnated, to the extent that it reverted to push-pull steam traction. From the War onwards the 'down line' was used for storage, the sole notable incident occurring on 17 June 1960 when a driver thinking the line was clear struck stored coaches, his engine falling down the embankment fortunately without injury. The final passenger train departed on 3 March 1962, the service withdrawn two days later. They would continue to run for a while empty though, as the line was used to train suburban DMU drivers. Goods traffic continued until 6 January 1964 when the Piddington-Bedford section was closed. Today part is incorporated in the *Stevington Country Walk*. Of the remainder in Northamptonshire the Piddington end transferred to the MoD, running until 1981, and at Northampton continued until 1994 when mothballed. While there have been discussions about reopening most of the original line, it appears unlikely to occur.

The Wycombe Railway Branches

The WR was the first to properly cross Buckinghamshire, establishing key connections before becoming part of the GWR (p.59). It equally spurred construction of two branch lines, further integrating rail travel across this area and ultimately leading to very different modern operations.

♦ *The Watlington & Princes Risborough Railway*

This first branch stemmed from the poor roads of Watlington (Oxfordshire). Seeking rail as an alternative, three proposals were submitted connecting to the GWR in Oxfordshire, the last successfully creating the 1866 Cholsey-Wallingford railway. It intended to run to Watlington via extensions, but a competing proposal from the Buckinghamshire side ended this plan. With assent in 1869 – well after the 1846 Gauge Act blocked further broad gauge in the area – the 'Watlington & Princes Risborough Railway' was from the outset a single-track standard gauge line. Originally the plan was a dual gauge section from Princes Risborough Station to the branch junction, but the ex-WR was regauged first. Rather than sharing this new standard gauge stretch it was decided to build a completely separate track running alongside the pre-existing route.

While landowners were often critical of early railways, here it was largely the opposite. Local residents the Earl of Macclesfield and Thomas Taylor, an affluent cotton manufacturer, not only supported the line but put up most of the construction costs, Taylor becoming a central figure within the company. Construction was rushed, the BoT twice being invited to inspect the line before completion, only finally opening on 15 August 1872 after a third inspection. In spite of their enthusiasm, from the outset the branch was a financial flop. Expenses continually exceeded income, worsened by rising debts owed to the GWR for operating the line, until in desperation the company even purchased unsuitable second-hand rolling stock to try and run it themselves. This may explain why one 1878 train accidentally departed without its coaches! Services comprised three trains daily, extended to five in 1875. That year the company offered to lease the line to the GWR; this led nowhere but trains began using their Princes Risborough Station (previously having a semi-independent platform). When the agreement to use GWR metals and the station expired in 1881 the GWR offered to take over the failing company. In spite of the financial difficulties this was plainly disliked, a new lease being discussed and Taylor only finally bringing the proposal to shareholders in 1883. The shareholders heavily criticised the takeover, not least as the GWR offer was less than half what it cost to build, but nonetheless the line was sold. The liquidator of the former company was none other than Thomas Taylor...

Chinnor Station (Oxfordshire), rebuilt 1994 – R. Jones.

The GWR discovered that the branch was very dilapidated, forcing investment in repairs. Returning to a three-train service, costs were kept down while an 1891 proposal to the GWR to extend the line to Wallingford was promptly declined. Things, however, began to look up. With the 1906 GWGCJR through Princes Risborough (p.37) there were considerably more connecting passenger trains, the branch equally rejuvenated with an additional daily train from 1900 and three new halts in 1906 (plus a fourth in 1925). Of these (and three other pre-existing stations after Princes Risborough) only Bledloe Bridge Halt was in Buckinghamshire.

Branch life continued largely unchanged through the Grouping and Nationalisation until 1951. From 5-7 March passenger services were temporarily replaced by bus, for an unusual reason. The regular fireman had been granted time off to get married, his relief had been called to national service and no other cover could be found! Trains only restarted when another driver volunteered to take on the duties. Although seeming light-hearted this reflected more serious issues, as on 19 June local newspapers announced that passenger services were to cease outright. The rise of road travel had severely reduced traffic but this decision triggered length debate, delaying closure. Ultimately the last passenger train ran on 29 June 1957. Goods continued, and while the Chinnor-Watlington stretch closed on 30 December 1960 this traffic only ended on 10 October 1966. Still the branch remained, now as a glorified siding serving the Chinnor Cement Works. Opened in 1908, its founder had a habit of whistling from his office over to the station when he wanted to catch a train, drivers commonly waiting for him before departing – late! It retained rail usage until 20 December 1989 when BR declared the hopper wagons obsolete.

Bledlow Bridge Halt, 1959 – Lamberhurst Collection.*

Although the branch was now closed, this was not the end. That same year enthusiasts formed the 'Chinnor and Princes Risborough Railway Association', running their first works train in 1991. The freehold was purchased in 1994 and on 20 August passenger trains returned. Opening extensions in 1995 and 1996, the line was reconnected to the national network on 21 February 2016 before being fully reinstated at Princes Risborough Station in 2018. Today it operates between these two stations with plans for further extension, re-establishing a traditional GWR branch line.

♦ *The Great Marlow Railway*

The second WR-connected branch ran from Bourne End Station ('Marlow Road' pre-1874) to Great Marlow ('Marlow' from 1899), a single track just under three miles long. First proposed to the GWR by local businesses in 1867, an Act was

Pannier No. 1369 on the Chinnor & Princes Risborough Railway – S. Mulligan.

Pannier No. 9421 at Bourne End Station, 1959 – B. Brooksbank.*

passed for the 'Great Marlow Railway' in 1868. Construction costs were supported by the GWR which operated the line for the local company, who in turn dealt with staff and maintenance. It opened on 28 June 1873, as with the Watlington branch being standard gauge from the outset. An extension to Henley-on-Thames was blocked by local opposition, and in 1897 the company was formally amalgamated into the GWR.

Although the reason is unknown – from a resident locomotive to an impromptu (and purportedly lost) race against a donkey cart – the service became known as the 'Marlow Donkey', a moniker that remains today. The line proved successful, not least due to the connecting WR being the area's only major railway. But the 1906 arrival of the GWGCJR created a shorter route, and with trains bypassing the lower ex-WR the branch suffered. In 1960 a camping coach was positioned at Bourne End and in 1962 the line was dieselised, but even so the decline continued, leading to Marlow Station being replaced in 1967 with a smaller terminus in the former goods yard.

Local usage continued though, particularly commuting, and although goods traffic ceased in 1966 the branch still had commercial value. Services continued into the 1970s with 20 trains daily (as they had since the 1930s), primarily branch-only or direct to Maidenhead. Connecting trains also ran to High Wycombe, passengers changing, but this was only ever a secondary destination and was withdrawn in 1970 when that portion of the ex-WR closed. From 2 May 1970 Bourne End consequently became a terminus junction and 'reversing station': trains from Maidenhead stopping there before reversing to Marlow. The surviving WR Maidenhead-Bourne End track thus became part of the branch itself. Today the hourly service under the 'Great Western Railway' franchise is complemented by two-train operation at peak times. A valued commuter line supported by the 'Marlow-Maidenhead Passengers' Association', it remains as a rare survivor that unwittingly lengthened as its main line connection diminished.

Cookham Station on the ex-WR, 1986 – B. Brooksbank.*

The Stratford-upon-Avon, Towcester & Midland Junction Railway

Connecting with the BNR (p.124) at Ravenstone Wood Junction near Olney (Buckinghamshire), this tiny strip of track was the end of a much longer and more significant west-east line spanning nearly 60 miles from Bedford to Stratford upon Avon, Banbury and Gloucester. Its convoluted history began with three companies' attempts to move Northamptonshire iron ore to Wales. First, in 1872 the 'Northampton & Banbury Junction Railway' opened a line from Blisworth via Towcester to Cockley Brake (Northamptonshire) on the LNWR Buckingham branch (p.47). The separate but closely-associated 'East & West Junction Railway' (EWJR) then built from Towcester to Stratford-upon-Avon (later extended via another company), opened in 1873. Lastly, affecting the Chilterns, the EWJR sponsored construction of the 'Stratford-upon-Avon, Towcester & Midland Junction Railway' from Towcester to Olney (before 1882 named the 'Easton Neston Mineral & Towcester Roade & Olney Junction Railway'). Authorised in 1879, operations were under a joint committee with the EWJR, the MR having running powers for goods and minerals, and trains ultimately sharing the BNR between Bedford and Olney. It opened to goods on 13 April 1891 and passengers on 1 December 1892, although the latter was so unsuccessful that it ended on this section by March 1893, becoming goods-only. Olney-Towcester passenger trains would only return with occasional race excursions from 1927.

Lightly built and failing financially, in 1891 the joint-working companies agreed to sell the line. Other than passing interest from the future GCR none were interested, so on 1 January 1909 they merged into the 'Stratford-upon-Avon & Midland Junction Railway' (SMJR), purchasing the Northampton-Banbury line in 1910. With this section running solely at night, Bristol-London MR goods traffic took advantage of the shorter route, but limited goods was worsened by withdrawal of banana and coal traffic c.1912. Wartime traffic failed to help, as did LMS attempts to encourage goods (diverting trains and reintroducing bananas). Finally recovering under BR (especially steel), 1950s Northamptonshire-Warwickshire passenger decline weakened the wider SMJR and despite ongoing use the Olney-Towcester section closed on 8 June 1958 – to allow construction of the M1 motorway. Severed shortly after, used as sidings until lifted in 1964, further SMJR section closures followed with the last iron ore traffic ceasing in 1967. Now mostly field borders, today the sole surviving portion is an MoD-run depot connection at Kineton (Warwickshire), a sorry end to a grand plan.

The Hemel Hempsted & London & North Western Railway

The MR had fewer Chilterns lines compared to other companies, with only one purpose-built branch. Connecting Hemel Hempstead in Hertfordshire to the MR at Harpenden it went through particularly convoluted development, subject to wider competition between companies. Even its nickname causes confusion; 'Puffing Annie' to some but best remembered as the 'Nickey Line'. Reasons abound for the name, from St Nicholas parish in Harpenden to the navvies' knickerbocker trousers, but the origin remains a mystery.

♦ *Protracted Efforts*

The LBR encountered landowner opposition during its development, forcing numerous deviations. At Hemel it skirted around the town, Boxmoor Station lying a mile from the centre. By 1862 this was plainly regretted, John Grover proposing a direct connection from station to town. Described by some as 'puny', another proposal simultaneously emerged for a longer line continuing via Redbourn to the GNR branch at Harpenden (p.76). The former gained support, being granted authorisation in 1863 as the 'Hemel Hempsted & London & North Western Railway', but landowner and other difficulties stalled construction. In the meantime the MR had been marching south, so the alternative proposition was reappraised. Plans for tunnels were unrealistic and Parliament rejected the scheme. Revisions, however, were approved in 1866 to extend the previously-authorised line under the MR to the GNR. Anticipating success, the company had already begun work in advance. Unfortunately the LNWR rapidly lost interest: the branch risked MR encroachment so a direct Boxmoor connection was blocked – instantly reducing it to a mere shuttle. Perhaps it was naive of the little company to think three fiercely competitive national companies would like a line transferring traffic between them!

Hemel Hempsted Station, c.1900 – Lamberhurst Collection.*

Construction was slow, changing contractors, with only the Boxmoor-Hemel section complete by 1871 (linked to the LNWR via an inconvenient turntable). A further extension to Chesham was considered but rejected, and financial issues arose – compounded by delays. Extensions were granted in 1870 and 1872, with further cost-cutting by relaxing standards under new 'light railway' legislation. With a national recession the MR was itself struggling, and a new branch offering custom from two towns was a lucrative notion even if concerned at possible LNWR incursion. They gave financial assistance in return for operating rights (previously to be the LNWR), but discussions dragged. It was agreed to rent the line but the MR charged for land at the junction and the company soon realised they had a poor deal, renegotiating in 1875. Landowner problems continued, particularly with the 'Boxmoor Trust' which greatly resented encroachment on the Common, but by 1876 the line was sufficiently complete for a MR inspection. The MR's amendments were charged to the company, including signalling. The company could only afford £500 towards this, so the MR only fitted the first £500 worth! Completion of the line was announced at short notice, the local newspaper sarcastically noting the LNWR, the lengthy build time, and the foolishness of competition. The intended GNR connection was ultimately never built.

The branch opened on 16 July 1877 amid great celebration, with luncheon, triumphal arch and band. The line's primary motivation was goods rather than passengers, particularly coal and straw plait, so the MR junction curved north towards Luton. Four Hemel-Luton trains ran daily, calling at Redbourn and Chiltern Green on the MR – the junction for London-bound travellers. This change meant the LNWR line was quicker overall, and the branch's shuttle format gave little advantage over the LNWR's new omnibus between Boxmoor and central Hemel, hindering branch passenger numbers. Some, however, preferred the branch over this monopoly. On 25 June 1886 the ailing company was absorbed into the MR, in part to end irksome rent dues. The 'Boxmoor Trust', however, claimed that new owners warranted a new land lease, the MR thus having to pay an additional toll. Growing to seven trains daily (reflecting doubled main line services by 1880), the collapse of locally-produced straw plait in the face of overseas imports resulted in a new passenger focus. Luton was now less important than London so the junction was realigned southwards in 1888, with Harpenden as the junction station and a St Albans through train until 1895.

At the other end, the line continued for a mile beyond Hemel Hempsted Station down to Boxmoor, never used for passengers. MR-LNWR rivalries ever-worsened, the branch a perceived threat, and not only was a connection unattained but the existing turntable link was removed in 1890 (the line fully severed c.1916). Beside LNWR fears, shortening the London route through bypassing St Pancras was not in the MR's interest either, potentially gifting traffic to their rival. Other than for stabling coal trains the track was scarcely used until post-1866 gasworks coal trains. Alongside Dickinson's paper this became the line's principal goods traffic. Despite urban development around Hemel passenger growth slowed in the 1890s. To maintain competition with the LNWR and their omnibus three new halts were opened in 1906 and a railmotor service introduced. This included Heath Park Halt, extending passenger services towards Boxmoor and unusually making a minor halt the terminus. Now running nine trains daily – four via Heath Park – the railmotors were a reasonable success, continuing until the 1920s. However, services reduced with WWI (six by 1918) and in 1914 first class was withdrawn, the start of a slow decline.

Heath Park Halt, c.1908 – Lamberhurst Collection.*

♦ *The Route*

The 9-mile single track had considerable civil engineering, requiring 23 bridges including a substantial three-arch viaduct at Marlowes, Hemel. Another traversed the A41 road, although this was somewhat slow and post-war buses occasionally stuck. If they could not be freed, a crane had to come and lift the bridge span! Even with lengthy earthworks, their construction hindered by the chalk terrain, the gradients were still some of the steepest in the country – a 1 in 37 incline near Harpenden often brought goods trains to a standstill and was comparable to the infamous 'Lickey Incline' (one possible reason for the 'Nickey' nickname). Tight curves added further challenges, ensuring a rough ride and in later years occasional derailments.

Meandering southwest, after Harpenden there were originally only stations at Hemel Hempsted (known as the 'Midland Station' to differentiate from Boxmoor; the 'a' in Hempstead only adopted by the railways in the 1950s) and Redbourn, later adding halts at Heath Park, Godwin's Siding, Beaumont's Halt and Roundwood Halt (1927). The line had several private sidings, notably 'Claydales Brickworks' (once having its own narrow gauge rail system) while at the Boxmoor end the line split in two: one part served the gasworks with the other being the ill-fated LNWR connection.

♦ *Not Standard Procedure…*

With an unorthodox history, tales of unauthorised practices are plentiful. When MR-LNWR rivalries were particularly bad, a MR locomotive was found having strayed into the Boxmoor yard. LNWR staff proceeded to remove the rails, essentially 'kidnapping' it! Sometimes colleagues were little better. An argument between guard and driver once led to the latter throwing the line tablet into a hedge and storming off home. Another driver kept chickens by the track, morning goods services surreptitiously stopping to pick up eggs. A guard similarly ensured train safety checks were always conducted near lineside pubs…

During WWII a short goods train stopped near Hemel to pin down brakes. The driver was known for excessive speed so the guard, losing patience, uncoupled the locomotive which shot off on its own. Gently rolling the train into the station he expected to find a terrified driver, only to discover from platform staff that while the engine shot through 'without much intention of stopping' the driver had actually enjoyed the ride! As for passengers, 'Puffing Annie' was so reliable that many left until the last minute to head for the station. The approaching whistle often triggered a veritable stampede, only ceasing with another whistle announcing departure. Some commuters would regularly be seen slowly trudging to Boxmoor Station, having missed their train!

Twice the branch saw filming, albeit minor. An LMS training film *Little & Often* required a Black Five Class running with a flat 'scenery' truck between it and the tender. Prior to main line filming this was tested for safety on the branch. Later Redbourn represented a fictional war-torn country in a 1966 episode of Elstree Studio's *The Baron*.

Under the Grouping the branch and both adjoining main lines came under the LMS but through trains never developed. As Harpenden grew with 'dormitory town' commuting in the 1920s-30s, Roundwood Halt opened to cater for nearby housing development. In 1929 the LMS experimented with extending the ex-LNWR omnibus, following the line from Boxmoor to Harpenden visiting each station. It proved a mixed blessing – a great success, the first week had more passengers than the train in a month. Rail services thus decreased from seven daily to four, often used by schoolchildren. Then in 1931 the branch hosted tests of the Karrier 'Ro-Railer'. This was a bus designed to expand services beyond the tracks: picking up passengers by road and driving to a nearby railway, after lowering built-in rail wheels it could continue along the branch. It had little success and was transferred to the SMJR in 1932 before withdrawal.

WWII brought increased traffic, from evacuees to tanks and supplies for the 'Great Ormond Street Hospital' relocated at Redbourn. In December 1943 the Middlesex Regiment was billeted in Hemel, boosting the limited passenger numbers. It would not last. Despite substantial post-war development around Hemel 'New Town', passenger traffic continued falling. Its inherent limitations from the MR-LNWR rivalry hampered local use, while the railway's own bus service had pushed passengers onto the roads. Goods operations were moved to Boxmoor, leaving the gasworks coal supply as the only substantial branch traffic left. A national coal shortage in winter 1946-7 triggered the temporary cessation of passenger trains, the last departing on 16 June 1947. They would never resume. Passengers only briefly returned with three railtours in 1957-8.

Goods services continued into Nationalisation, the branch surviving on two daily trains. A permanent link to the ex-LNWR was finally installed in 1948 to enable WCML access to the gasworks, but it only saw fleeting use c.1959-60. Urban redevelopment triggered the removal of the Hemel-Boxmoor embankment (severing the line), closure of Heath Park Halt in 1959, and the demolition of the Marlowes Viaduct in 1960. Closures continued with Hemel and Redbourn stations (as goods depots) in 1963, goods services officially ceasing in July 1964 (Godwin's Halt closing) although traffic stopped some time beforehand. But there

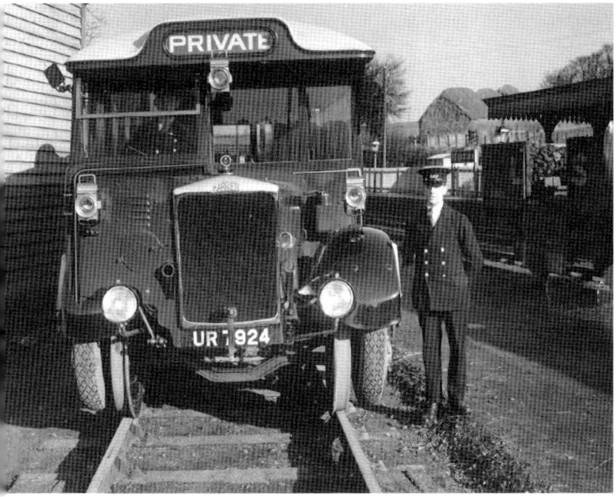

The experimental Ro-Railer at Redbourn, 1931 – Author's Collection.

'Hemelite' 04 Class D2203; ex-Wisbech Tramway, she is the original Mavis from Thomas the Tank Engine – *Author, with permission from the Embsay & Bolton Abbey Steam Railway.*

was to be a stay of execution. The former 'Claydales Brickworks' began post-War manufacture of clinker blocks, in 1958 being taken over and upgraded under the tradename 'Hemelite'. BR-hauled traffic commenced in 1959 and after the branch's closure the surviving 6-mile section to Harpenden was purchased on 30 April 1968, becoming the first British railway line privately taken over from BR. Operated independently, retaining partial use of Redbourn, Roundwood Halt and Beaumont's Halt, there were struggles with maintenance access and vandalism but trains kept running. Marking the 1977 centenary, in 1979 BR's main line upgrades reached Harpenden. 'Hemelite' could not justify the cost of points replacement, so on 24 July the branch was severed outright and deliveries turned to roads. Lifted in 1982, the branch was no more.

♦ *Surviving Traces*

Little is left in central Hemel, although faint traces of Heath Park Halt remain. Much of the trackbed opened in 1985 as the *Nickey Line* cycleway, Roundwood Halt platform also surviving, while sections were used in the Redbourn bypass road. The line is still fondly remembered, some wistfully claiming the sound of a whistle in town is 'the Ghost of Puffing Annie'...

Skirting Buckinghamshire: The West Drayton Branches

Almost entirely outside Buckinghamshire, skirting its border, the history of these connected lines nonetheless relates to the Chilterns and nearby branches, having partial success despite inter-company animosity.

♦ *The GWR Uxbridge-West Drayton Branch*

Uxbridge was a notable stagecoach town but suffered after opposing the LBR and GWR. In 1846 the 'Great Western & Uxbridge Railway' gained assent: a branch to the nearby main line at West Drayton (Middlesex). Local investment, however, was so reluctant that in 1847 the promoters appealed to the GWR directly, the line being taken over before even built. Construction was further delayed, only opening on 8 September 1856. As with early GWR lines it was originally broad gauge – an exception to 1846 restrictions – but was regauged in 1871, taking only four days to complete. Lord Ebury's 1862 Rickmansworth branch (p.101) had intended to meet it, but this was never achieved.

Later known as the Uxbridge Vine Street Branch, this entire line was just outside Buckinghamshire. Traffic was plentiful, services increasing to include a through-train to Paddington and some 45 trains daily by 1913. Doubled in 1880 plus a single 1904 intermediate station, a competing 1901 tram system, 1904 MET branch and another GWR branch in 1907 (p.138) reduced passenger numbers. None of these branches connected, hindering them all to some degree. Railmotors were introduced in 1913 but service numbers decreased by the 1950s. Traffic plainly suffered even with 1958 railcars for it was referenced in Beeching's Report as having already been withdrawn. Branch passenger services ended on 10 September 1962, being singled for goods-only operation before largely closing on 13 July 1964. The final spur to an oil works remained in use until 8 January 1979.

♦ *The Staines & West Drayton Railway*

The Uxbridge line's main relevancy to the Chilterns was its GWR connection. In 1863 a line was proposed between West Drayton and Staines on the LSWR. Failing, a second 1866 attempt expired after insufficient financial support. A third attempt in 1873 created the 'Staines & West Drayton Railway', still requiring two extensions due to financial issues and route alterations. Although the company pushed for GWR support the latter was reticent, fearful of antagonising the LSWR – which had already objected to any broad gauge incursion and refused access to their Staines Station. It was only in 1882 that the GWR finally agreed to operate the line, on the understanding that there would be an independent terminus.

A single track built to standard gauge on LSWR insistence, following the River Colne, it originally had one intermediate station at Colnbrook (near Slough) – the only part within Buckinghamshire. Rather than a direct connection to the GWR a section of the Uxbridge branch was utilised, trains heading north on its track before diverging and turning south under the main line towards Staines. However, construction problems arose. A bridge over the Wraysbury River was

The former Colnbrook Station, 1986 – B. Brooksbank.*

The surviving Colnbrook track at West Drayton Station, 2007 – N. Cox.*

so poorly built that it collapsed before the line opened, while to save money the Staines terminus was converted from a Georgian house. More pressingly, the first builder was dismissed leading to a legal battle that the company lost, while the threat of additional legal action from the second builder damaged finances further. In solution, the two builders built part each.

The first section from West Drayton Station to Colnbrook opened on 9 August 1884, the completed line to Staines on 2 November 1885. As the majority shareholder, supporting the company's finances particularly through the legal proceeding, the GWR took over the branch outright on 1 July 1900. Passenger traffic was reasonable at first, the branch enabling easy commuting as a link between the GWR and LSWR (although only physically during WWII and the 1980s; p.92), but the main focus was goods. Even so, by the 1920s new halts were added to encourage passengers, with five additional stations by 1961 (including Colnbrook Estate Halt, Buckinghamshire). The shared section of Uxbridge branch was doubled in 1940.

Remaining with the GWR through the Grouping, rising post-war road use led to declining traffic, worsened by the sparsely-populated area, and goods traffic beyond Colnbrook ceased on 2 November 1953. Despite 1958 dieselisation, 1963 saw the branch included in the Beeching Report. On 27 March 1965 the final passenger train departed, the service ending two days later. The line itself, however, gained a lifeline. A fuel oil depot was built in the former Staines good yard in 1964, reviving goods traffic. This remained until 1981 when the lower part was severed by the M25 motorway, the depot gaining a link to the ex-LSWR line (closed a decade later). A connecting spur was finally laid linking the Staines and Windsor branches, remaining until 1991. Only one passenger train ever used it: the 1981 *Farewell to Staines West Branch* railtour. Ironically, by using this spur the Special never travelled to Staines West Station.

♦ *The Lines Today*

While heavily segmented, much still remains. The shortened Staines branch to Colnbrook (including the formerly-shared part of the Uxbridge branch) remains open to goods, helping to construct Heathrow Airport's Terminal 5 and still supplying aviation fuel. Although much has been repurposed parts of the trackbeds are walkable, while a section of the Uxbridge route is now a nature reserve. In 2009 a Heathrow support line was proposed, aiming to reintroduce the Staines line, but this plan ended in 2011. Since then the branch has been included in plans for the ex-LSWR Windsor branch under 'Airtrack-Lite', connecting them in what would be an extended version of the original line. Still under discussion, it may be many years before trains return...

The GER Edmonton-Cheshunt Branch

A main line in all but name, this 'branch' in southeast Hertfordshire acted with other Lea Valley lines to create a shortcut for the ex-GER West Anglia Main Line, this part now known as the 'Southbury Loop' ('Churchbury Loop' until 1960). It began with the ECR Enfield branch via Edmonton, opened in 1849. Becoming part of the GER in 1862, this was met by a new double-track line in 1872 from Bethnal Green to Edmonton, shortening the distance and tapping into local suburban expansion. With these in place and growing prospective traffic, another extension re-joining the main line would enable the circuitous Stratford route to be bypassed. This was first considered in the 1860s, albeit abandoned, and with the idea resurfacing powers were granted in 1882 for a connecting Edmonton-Cheshunt branch. Three stations were built, only Theobalds Grove being in Hertfordshire.

Commencing construction in 1889 the Cheshunt line opened on 1 October 1891, but the anticipated housing development failed to materialise and traffic was poor. This was exacerbated by few trains actually going to Liverpool Street, most services terminating at White Hart Lane on the Hackney Downs line. Worse still, Waltham Cross gained a tram system in 1908, dropping branch passenger levels by half. Goods conversely were more stable, bricks and market garden produce in particular, with the area beginning to industrialise. As little tank engines shuttled ever-emptier auto-trains, the GER took what was for its time a highly unusual action: on 1 October 1909 passenger services were withdrawn. Closures were then so rare that the President of the Board of Trade, Winston Churchill, was questioned on it in Parliament.

Thereafter the branch was goods-only, traffic increasing substantially during WWI. 'Waltham Abbey Royal Gunpowder Mills' was by the Cheshunt junction, munitions consequently a major load. But with a shortage of shells culminating in a public scandal in 1915, output needed to be increased. This probably contributed to the Government requesting the GER to reinstate passenger services, the main users being munitions workers. Services restarted on 1 March 1915 (with a new temporary halt in Enfield opened in 1916) but this was withdrawn again on 1 July 1919. By the 1920s housing development

Cheshunt Station, 2009 – S. Craven.*

had finally begun but the now-LNER branch remained goods-only – so minor that it was worked as a single track, the 'up line' used for wagon storage. Nonetheless, it retained value as a diversion route, particularly when the main line flooded or was damaged, especially during WWII. The branch itself did not escape unharmed – Theobalds Grove Station was damaged in 1945 by a nearby V2 rocket attack. The 'Gunpowder Mills' remained a notable munitions manufacturer until 1943, the branch likely playing a diminishing role.

After the War there was another spate of housing development, and in the 1950s BR enacted plans from 1944: electrification and a new passenger service. Commencing on 21 November 1960, this preceded electrification of the main line itself and proved highly successful, becoming a busy suburban line. Goods traffic, however, decreased with yards closing by 1970. Worked by 'Network SouthEast' and various post-Privatisation companies under the *Lea Valley Lines*, on 31 May 2015 the Loop transferred to TFL as part of 'London Overground'. Different services have run since electrification with the constituent Loop branches amalgamated into one, including a 1964 London-Broxbourne train partially fulfilling the original 'alternate main line' intention. Since 2015 EMUs traverse up to Cheshunt and peak times see some Hertford East branch services (p.69). Compared to other Chiltern branches it is ironic how this early withdrawal ultimately became one of its busiest survivors...

The GWR Denham-Uxbridge Branch

Mostly outside Buckinghamshire, this stalled project's history links with other nearby lines; the victim of excessive rail construction through competition. Uxbridge gained its first branch in 1856 (p.135), but with suburban growth it soon attracted others. An 1864 WR proposal would have linked it to High Wycombe; the GWR took this project over but abandoned it in preference of their Marlow branch (p.127). However, in 1898 they gained an Act for a second Uxbridge line south from the GWGCJR to loop around Uxbridge before meeting the West Drayton branch. Under construction from 1900, unfortunately the 'Harrow and Uxbridge Railway' was authorised in 1897, opened on 4 July 1904 –

Denham Station, 1990 – B. Brooksbank.*

beating the GWR to completion. Now with MET competition the GWR changed their plans, pausing construction and building a temporary terminus, opened on 1 May 1907. Partially on a viaduct the branch stopped in mid-air, ready for construction to continue southwards.

With competing branches and tramways, these alternatives resulted in such little passenger traffic that the line was an almost instant failure. This was compounded by no initial goods facilities, only gaining a small yard in 1914. Trains ran between Uxbridge High Street and Denham (Buckinghamshire), the only two stations, with some continuing to Gerrards Cross on the GWGCJR (the branch itself remaining solely under the GWR). At Denham a triangle junction was built, although the eastern part was closed during WWI. The line had not been extended since opening and, despite land having already been purchased, in 1914 its Act was allowed to lapse. Thus in only seven years the branch had failed so badly that its primary purpose had been abandoned.

Now operating in this new but minor capacity, even with added goods work traffic was poor. The line was singled in 1916 and as a wartime economy on 1 January 1917 passenger services were withdrawn. Goods traffic continued, and surprisingly a weekday passenger service was reinstated on 3 May 1920. This plainly had little impact, as by 1937 the service comprised only a single carriage auto-train. On 1 September 1939 passenger services were again withdrawn, never to return. Remaining under goods operation through to BR, the 'temporary' terminus remained until demolished in 1955 and the non-yard tracks removed, having one final use with a 1954 enthusiast special. The last good train ran on 24 February 1964 and the remaining structures were demolished by the mid-1970s. Little remains today, although part of the trackbed forms a nature walk through Denham Country Park. One wonders if today's walkers exceed the railway's former passenger numbers.

The Watford MET Branch

Competing from the outset with the LNWR and repeatedly stymied in its extension attempts, this last Hertfordshire branch never matched its intentions. Hindered by position, it nonetheless continues operation as a MET commuter link with future aspirations.

♦ *Troubled Beginnings*

In 1895 the 'Watford Tradesmen's Association' first suggested to the MET the potential for a Watford branch. Little resulted, as with a 1903 proposal from Watford Urban District Council, and it was only after a petition in 1906 that the idea was forwarded to the MGCJR. Knowing of the LNWR's Croxley plan (p.102) greater interest was shown, an Act being passed in 1912. This required two amendments though. Watford Council had recently purchased the former Cassiobury Estate as a park so were against a railway cutting through it. Consequently, instead of the intended site the terminus was built in Cassiobury Avenue by the goods yard – an area ironically then known as 'The Wilderness'. Secondly, the LNWR insisted that the track level be raised to allow for any

Ninety years of the Watford MET branch, 2015 – P. Hodge.

The Watford MET branch over the GJC – Author.

potential extension of their Croxley branch.

By the time these were resolved the GCR had entered financial difficulties. The MET considered building it alone but the GCR maintained interest. Still stalling even after competing *Bakerloo* trains began running into Watford Junction (p.83), the GCR blamed WWI for yet further delays. It was only with post-war government aid that work finally started in 1922. The GCR was still doubtful and questioned traffic levels, but the MET assured that it would be considerable. Construction had challenges, not least the Depression, and following requests from the Council and British Legion branch many local unemployed men were hired for the project. Complexities meant the original 1924 completion date was unreachable even with double shifts, and it was only on 2 October 1925 that a Ministry of Transport inspection could be undertaken. Previously in 1912 the dedicated 'Watford Joint Railway Committee' was formed to operate the line.

♦ *The Route*

Electrified from new, the double track passed northeast through Croxley Station ('Croxley Green' until 1949) to Watford. Heavy civil engineering was required with cuttings plus a substantial embankment and bridge over the River Gade and GJC. The MET junction formed a triangle, the lower 'Watford South Curve' being the main route towards London. The 'Watford North Curve' conversely diminished operationally after the 1934 cessation of Watford-Rickmansworth shuttles (partially due to bus competition). Nearby was the connection to 'Croxley Tip', a former gravel quarry used as a landfill for old ballast.

♦ *Operation and Continuation*

The branch opened to a civic welcome on 31 October 1925, services commencing from 2 November. With 35 electric trains daily to Baker Street and another 35 steam services to Marylebone, the *Watford Observer* declared that this was 'likely to have a much greater effect on the town than is at present realised'. Unfortunately, GCR fears were well founded as passenger numbers were limited; GCR trains were withdrawn during the 1926 General Strike and never reinstated. The key issue was Watford Station's location – a mile from the town centre in, at the time, a largely undeveloped area. Such was its remoteness that only a week after opening the MET arranged for a connecting bus service. Goods traffic conversely was sufficient to justify purchasing five road lorries for deliveries, and by the mid-1930s there was a regular seasonal traffic in bulbs to the Continent.

Croxley Green MET Station, designed in the Arts and Crafts style – J. Reilly.

By 1931 houses were starting to develop around the station, although not with MET involvement. While aiding the branch, the MET still looked towards central Watford, in 1927 purchasing a tea rooms on Watford High Street. An ideal station location, two potential subterranean routes were planned: under Cassiobury Park or skirting to the south. Neither was built, the High Street premises being sold in 1936. Goods traffic ceased in November 1966 (although officially that October), and by 1989 there were services every 15 minutes. The line remains in full use under TFL, today surrounded by commuter suburbs. The Watford terminus has been threatened several times with potential closure, to be truncated as part of the 'Croxley Rail Link' (p.105), but with this still unresolved the branch is likely to remain unchanged into the future.

Electrified former MET steam carriages, c.1930 – Author's Collection.

Exceptions

These railways formed the national network within the Chilterns but they were not alone, being supplemented by tramways, internal factory railways and a host of industrial narrow-gauge lines. One deserves particular mention, returning to the railways' earliest days. The LBR is widely considered the Chilterns' first railway, but technically this is incorrect. In 1825 – the same year as the ground-breaking 'Stockton & Darlington Railway' – a 1.5-mile 'railroad' was built in Cheshunt to transport bricks to the River Lea. Based on the patent of Henry Palmer, trolleys pulled by horses ran atop a single elevated wood-and-iron 'rail', operating for several years before being superseded. But there is a twist to its history. When first opened, 25 June 1825, rather than carrying bricks locals clambered aboard instead for a ride. As a result of this opening day stunt the Chilterns has the unlikely accolade of hosting the world's first passenger-carrying monorail…

The Chilterns Rail Network Today

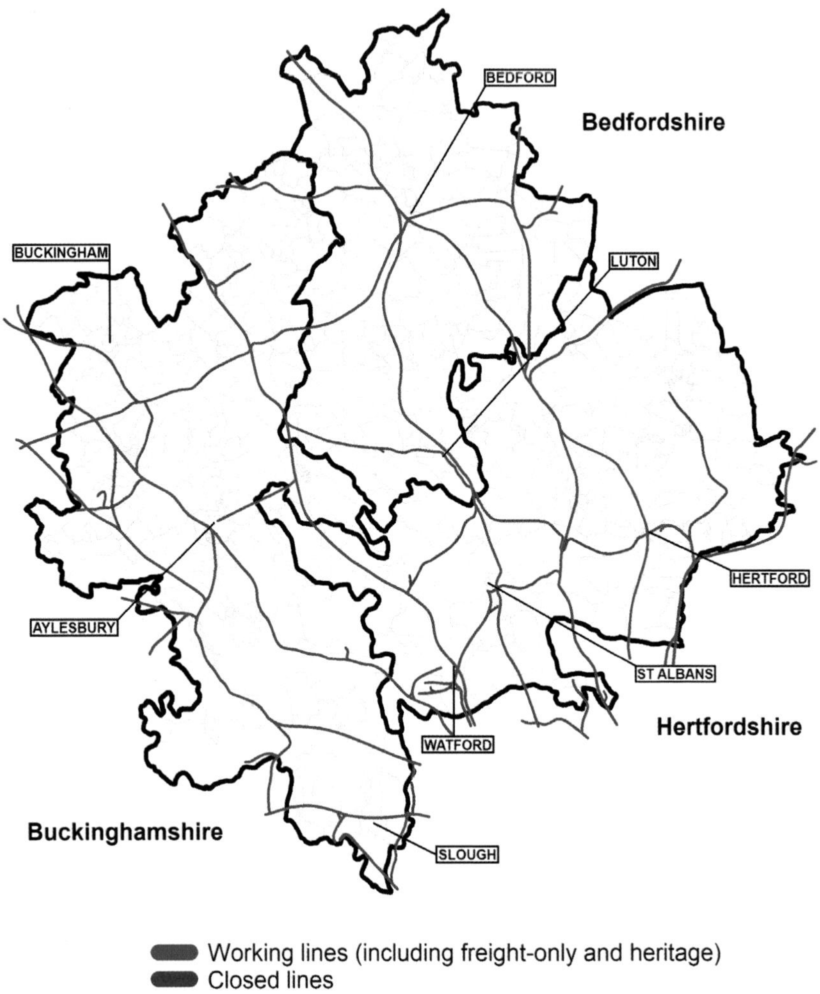

Departures and Arrivals

The effects of railway development across the Chilterns were marked. While some areas prospered, in turn encouraging cyclical transport development, other communities – particularly the most rural without rail links – were brought to their knees. There was also a broader impact: supported by railway-facilitated changes the Chilterns played a notable role in national history, from Prime Ministers to codebreakers. While their effects were neither uniform nor always positive, railways unquestionably helped transform this region.

Such changes may be considered a Victorian phenomenon, however, their impacts were arguably even greater in the 1950s–60s with road dominance and Dr Beeching. Hardly any recall positive effects of these though, instead seen as the death knell for many smaller communities. But as their history reveals, few of the outright closures were actually directly due to Beeching's Report – only five lines – blame for the rest often being attributed even when already long suspended. Nonetheless, the damage was done. While some lines were indeed unprofitable, their loss still impacted on society and wider logistics. Removing west-east lines in particular severed accessibility; now only possible by a London detour or a slower bus. With unemployment, reduced accessibility and increased road congestion, small wonder that the 'Axe' remains one of the most popularly-vilified actions of modern domestic history. Fortunately survival as walks or preservation groups ensures their ongoing appreciation.

But what of the future? Closure has given way to construction – the first in the Chilterns since 1925. One of the most debated civil projects of recent years, *High Speed 2* aims to provide a rapid passenger-only line between London and Birmingham (the Manchester and Leeds arm cancelled). Over ten years of planning it gained notoriety for division over every aspect, from environmental impacts to cost. On one side it could be seen as a duplication of the original LBR, right down to its limiting terminus-terminus focus. Conversely, it may help alleviate the WCML and create a new cross-country artery. Either way it will remain a sensitive topic for years to come.

Whether considering their past, present or future, the railways are an important element of Britain's society, economy and culture. Those of the Chilterns ranged from pivotal national arteries to quaint little lines meandering through the countryside. All had an effect on this area, helping make it what we know today. From the pioneering days of steam on into the future, long may they continue.

All Clear: broad-gauger Firefly *from the footpate – Author, with permission from Didcot Railway Centre.*

Bibliography

C.J. Allen, *The Great Eastern Railway* (London, 1975).
C. Awdry, *Encyclopaedia of British Railway Companies* (Frome, 1990).
F. Booker, *The Great Western Railway: A New History* (Newton Abbot, 1980).
J. & H. Cannon, *The Nickey Line* (Chesham, 1977).
F. Cockman, *The Railway Age in Bedfordshire*, Publications of the Bedfordshire Historical Record Society, 53 (Ampthill, 1974).
F. Cockman, *The Railways of Buckinghamshire from the 1830s* (Aylesbury County Record Office, 1971).
F. Cockman, *The Railways of Hertfordshire* (Hertford, 1978).
R. Davies & M.D. Grant, *Forgotten Railways of the Chilterns and Cotswolds*, (Newton Abbot, 1975).
M. Dawes, *The End of the Line: the Story of the Railway Service to the Great Northern London Cemetery* (Barnet, 2003).
M. Eckett, *Signals – A Railway Miscelleny* (Copt Hewick, 2008).
L. Ford, *Wickham of Ware – a History of D. Wickham and Company Ltd Railcar Manufacturers* (Ware, 2003).
C. Foxell, *The Story of the Met & GC Joint Line* (Amersham, 2001).
J. Giles, R. Jeavons, M. Martin, D. Smith & R. Smith, *Wheathampstead Railway Recollections* (Wheathampstead, 1995).
D.I. Gordon, *A Regional History of the Railways of Great Britain, Vol. 5 The Eastern Counties* (Newton Abbot, 1976).
G. Goslin, *The London Extension of the Midland Railway: A History of the St Pancras – Bedford Route* (Caernarfon, 1994).
F.W. Goudie & D. Stuckey, *West of Watford: Watford Metropolitan & the L.M.S. Croxley Green and Rickmansworth Branches* (Bracknall, 1990).
A.E. Grigg, *Town of Trains: Bletchley and the Oxbridge Line* (Buckingham, 1980).
C. Grinling, *The History of the Great Northern Railway, 1845-1922* (London, 1966).
C. Hamilton Ellis, *Four Main Lines* (London, 1950).
C. Hamilton Ellis, *The Midland Railway* (London, 1953).
P. Hodge, *The Hertford Loop* (London, 1976).
M. Home, *The Metropolitan Line* (Harrow Weald, 2003).
S. Jenkins, *The Great Western & Great Central Joint Railway* (Usk, 1978).
S. Jenkins, *The Watford to St Albans Branch* (Usk, 1990).
K. Jones, *The Wotton Tramway* (Tarrant Hinton, 1974).
A. Jowett, *Jowett's Railway Atlas of Great Britain & Ireland* (Wellingborough, 1989).
R. Leleux, *A Regional History of the Railways of Great Britain, Vol. 9 The East Midlands* (Newton Abbot, 1976).
C. Maggs, *Branch Lines of Buckinghamshire* (Stroud, 2000).
Sir F. Markham, *History of Milton Keynes and District Vol. 2* (Luton, 1986).
F. Newman, *The Socio-Economic Impacts of the coming of the Railways to Hertfordshire, Bedfordshire and Buckinghamshire, 1838–1900* (PhD dissertation, Hatfield, University of Hertfordshire, 2015).
O.S. Nock, *The London and North Western Railway* (London, 1960).
L. Oppitz, *Lost Railways of the Chilterns* (Newbury, 1991).
The Reshaping of British Railways Part 1: Report (London, 1963).
S.N. Pike, *Mile by Mile On Britain's Railways* (London, 2011).
P. Richards & B. Simpson, *A History of the London and Birmingham Railway Vol. 1 and 2* (Witney, 2004).
K. Scholey, *Bedfordshire's Lost Railways* (Glasgow, 2003).
K. Scholey, *Buckinghamshire's Lost Railways* (Glasgow, 2004).
K. Scholey, *Hertfordshire's Lost Railways* (Glasgow, 2003).
J. Simmons, *The Railway in Town and Country 1830-1914* (Newton Abbot, 1986).
B. Simpson, *A History of the Metropolitan Railway Vol. 3* (Witney, 2005).
B. Simpson, *The Aylesbury Railway* (Sparkford, 1989).
B. Simpson, *The Brill Tramway* (Oxford, 1985).
B. Simpson, *The Dunstable Branch* (Banbury, 1998).
B. Simpson, *The Wolverton to Newport Pagnell Branch* (Banbury, 1995).
R. Taylor & B. Anderson, *The Hatfield & St Albans Branch* (Oxford, 1988).
B. West, *The Trainmakers – the Story of Wolverton Works* (Buckingham, 1982).
G. Woodward, *The Hatfield, Luton & Dunstable Railway (and on to Leighton Buzzard)* (Usk, 1977).